CONTENTS

T0082327

EDINBURGH

Venerable, dramatic Edinburgh, the showcase capital of Scotland, is a historic, cultured and cosmopolitan city, regularly topping polls as the most desirable place to live in the United Kingdom. Of course, the locals have always known as much, savouring a skyline built on a string of extinct volcanoes and rocky crags that rises from the generally flat landscape of the Lothians, with the sheltered shoreline of the Firth of Forth to the north. Edinburgh-born author Robert Louis Stevenson declared of his precipitous city: "No situation could be more commanding for the head of a kingdom; none better chosen for noble prospects." The Scottish capital's grand, imposing aesthetic might have long stolen the limelight but today the city's grittier corners are stepping out of the shadows as they are reimagined as cool new neighbourhoods.

Descending Arthur's Seat towards the city centre

ROUGH GUIDES

POCKET **ROUGH GUIDE**
EDINBURGH

Written and researched by
BRENDON GRIFFIN AND KEITH MUNRO
This edition updated by
JOANNA REEVES

Along with its beauty, Edinburgh is blessed by its brevity, a wonderfully compact city ripe for exploration on foot. The centre has two distinct parts: the unrelentingly medieval Old Town, with its tortuous alleys and tightly packed closes, and the dignified, eighteenth-century Grecian-style New Town. Dividing the two are Princes Street Gardens, which run roughly east to west under the shadow of Edinburgh Castle. Clinging to the hill that rolls down from the fairy-tale Castle to the royal Palace of Holyroodhouse, the Old Town preserves all the key landmarks from its role as a historic capital, augmented by the dramatic and unusual Scottish Parliament building and the redevelopment of both Holyrood Road and the area around Market Street and New Street just off the Royal Mile. A few hundred yards away, a tantalizing glimpse of wild Scotland can be had in Holyrood Park, a sprawling pocket of wilderness bang in the centre of the city, dominated by Arthur's Seat, the largest and most impressive of the city's volcanoes.

In the National Gallery of Scotland

Among Edinburgh's many museums, the exciting National Museum of Scotland shelters ten thousand of Scotland's most precious artefacts, while the National Gallery of Scotland and its offshoot, the Scottish National Gallery of Modern Art, house two of Britain's finest collections of paintings.

In August, around a million visitors flock to the city for the Edinburgh Festival, in fact a series of separate festivals (see page 26) that makes up the largest arts extravaganza in the world. On a less elevated theme, the city's vast array of distinctive pubs, allied to its brewing and distilling traditions, makes it an unrivalled drinking

What's new

Whisky tourism is having a bit of a moment in Edinburgh. From interactive tours to whisky festivals and fancy bars, Scotland's distilleries are turning their hand to exciting ventures to attract a younger generation. In 2021, Johnnie Walker Princes Street (see page 82) opened in the centre of Edinburgh: an eight-storey Art Deco whisky emporium offering immersive tours involving live performances, light shows, and tastings in its shiny new bar, the *Explorers' Bothy*. Over on the other side of the Castle, The Scotch Whisky Experience (see page 40) is planning a £3 million revamp, while the Holyrood Distillery (see page 66) – which opened in 2019 – hosted the inaugural Mash Up in 2022, an annual festival centred on whisky, gin, beer and street food. Further afield in Perthshire, the Glenturret distillery – a popular day-trip from the capital – was given a luxury spin by new Swiss owners Lalique in 2019, with revamped experiential tours, a Michelin-starred restaurant and a boutique shop stocking a 50-year-old single malt in a black-crystal decanter for a bank-breaking £50,000.

Edinburgh castle dusted with snow

city. Its four universities, plus several colleges, mean that there is a youthful presence for most of the year. Beyond the city centre, the liveliest area is Leith, the city's medieval port, a thriving culinary quartier with a heady, beardy mix of traditional and cutting-edge bars, upmarket seafood restaurants and seasonal foragers. Snapping at its heels for the title of most surprising foodie destination, North Berwick is home to a growing crop of independent coffee shops and roasters, unassuming sea-to-plate haunts and an eco-conscious gin distillery. This small town is part of the wider rural hinterland of Edinburgh, known as the Lothians, which mixes rolling countryside and attractive country towns with some impressive historic ruins.

In East Lothian, blustery clifftop paths lead to the romantic battlements of Tantallon Castle, while the most famous sight in Midlothian is the mysterious fifteenth-century Rosslyn Chapel. To the northwest of the city, both the dramatic steel geometry of the Forth Rail Bridge and the graceful towers of the Queensferry Crossing (the longest bridge of its kind in the world) are best viewed by walking across the Forth Road bridge, starting at South Queensferry.

When to visit

Being closer to sunny East Lothian than the sodden west coast, Edinburgh's main climatic drawback is not so much precipitation as biting wind. Even in summer, sea breezes can keep temperatures down, as can the *haar*, mist that sometimes rolls in after a spell of fine weather. In recent years, March, April and May have seen some of the best and most prolonged spells of warm sunshine and blue skies (enhanced, in May at least, by wonderfully long days and short nights), though the implications for climate change are less than wonderful. The summer months of June, July and especially August (average max 17–19°) are notoriously unpredictable and often wet, as Fringe regulars know only too well. While winters are generally cold (average max 7–10°) and gloomy, you can still be lucky and hit upon a gorgeous few days of crisp sunshine. Crowds of tourists now throng Edinburgh year-round, reaching a peak during the Fringe, Christmas and especially New Year.

Where to...

Shop

Edinburgh's shopping scene may be small but it packs a punch. Just off Princes Street, the new St James Quarter is making waves. If labels are your thing, you'll find enough here and in nearby George Street to blow your entire travel budget. For vintage gear, independent designers, comics, antiquarian books and even fossils, the Old Town is your oyster, especially Candlemaker Row, Victoria Street, the Grassmarket and West Port. Stockbridge (especially St Stephen Street) and Newington are also good bets for quirky boutiques and antique shops. For delis and artisan food shopping, again the Old Town and Stockbridge come up trumps, as do Marchmont, Bruntsfield and Morningside (for food markets, see page 7). And last but not least, it may not surprise you to learn that the Royal Mile is the place to load up on malt whisky and get kilted-out with some tartan.

OUR FAVOURITES: Lighthouse Bookshop see page 60. W. Armstrong see page 60. Mr Wood's Fossils see page 60.

Eat

As you'd expect for a capital city, Edinburgh's exceptionally dynamic eating scene offers Scotland's most comprehensive dining, with everything from cheapie cosmopolitan pies to fresh-from-the-quayside seafood to hipster pop-up and seasonally foraged heaven, with plenty of Michelin stars to go round. Lunch is usually served between noon and 2pm, and is the best time to nab a bargain in the city's more upscale restaurants, particularly Michelin-star holders, taking advantage of the gourmand two- or three-course set menus without the sky-high price tag. In the evening, restaurants start filling up from around 7pm and serve till 10/11pm. The sheer weight of Edinburgh's tourist numbers, however, means that many places serve food round the clock, seven days a week, and are packed round the clock; don't ever assume you can simply turn up and nab a table. Generally, the Old Town remains the locus of traditional, pricey Scottish and French-influenced cuisine, ever more locally sourced, while Leith, naturally, is home to the most renowned seafood, and, increasingly, the most exciting new ventures.

OUR FAVOURITES: Heron see page 111. The Lookout by Gardener's Cottage see page 82. Tupiniquim see page 9.

Drink

Perhaps even more than a gourmet's paradise, Edinburgh is a drinker's shangri-la, with almost every variety of alcoholic beverage available, and a bewildering array of premises to serve them in. Very generally speaking, the Old Town is your best bet for a traditional Scottish pub; Newington is studded with boisterous student bars; the West End, Stockbridge and New Town specialize in wine bars and quirky one-offs, while Leith and Portobello are hipster central. Edinburgh licensing laws are gloriously liberal, at least for the UK, with most places open till at least 1am and some till 3am, and most of the city free from the byelaws in force in other Scottish regions forbidding drinking in public.

OUR FAVOURITES: The Waverley see page 53. Café Royal Circle Bar see page 83. Teuchters Landing see page 113.

The main ingredient: al fresco Edinburgh

From Michelin-starred restaurants to independent cafés and sea-to-plate restaurants, Edinburgh has a thriving food scene. A new generation of inventive chefs is giving a contemporary twist to classic Scottish dishes, showcasing the bounty of the mountains and the lochs. From Shetland Lamb and Orkney beef to Stornoway black pudding and Loch Fyne oysters, there is a commitment to quality native produce and ethical sourcing. The drive towards everything artisan, organic, seasonal and foraged and local has inevitably gone hand in hand with a flowering of farmers' markets, street food, kiosks, pop-ups and festivals. We've listed the most prominent examples below, but the dynamism of the Edinburgh scene means that the best culinary experiences can often be the most spontaneous and unexpected, especially during the Fringe when all manner of wild and wonderful pop-ups bloom for a few short weeks: keep your eyes peeled and your nose trained.

EDINBURGH FARMERS' MARKET

MAP PAGE 96

Castle Terrace. www.edinburghfarmersmarket.co.uk. Sat 9am–2pm

The trademark blue-and-white striped awnings shelter everything you'd expect from such a veteran player: handmade cheese, organic charcuterie, grass-fed meat, seasonal organic veg, award-winning fruit wines and more, plus demos by locavore-leaning and sustainability-driven non-profit Edinburgh Slow Food.

EDINBURGH FOOD FESTIVAL

MAP PAGE 124

George Square, Newington. www.edfoodfest.com. Late July

The benches of lovely George Square Gardens are warmed up in late July with this pre-Fringe affair run by Assembly, part of the Edinburgh Festival Fringe. Aiming to stimulate grey matter as well as taste buds, with plenty of expert Scottish foodie debate, entertainment and demos alongside the specialist comestibles. Free.

KAYS BAR

MAP PAGE 102

OMNi Centre, Leith St. www.edinburgh-street-food.com. Daily noon–11pm.

Edinburgh's first permanent daily street-food market opened in 2023 by the OMNi Centre and just a short hop from the new St James Quarter. A huddle of foodie favourites, including reimagined fine-dining spot *Junk* and bao specialists *Bundits*, has set up shop in the 900-square-metre enclave, which opens out onto an urban garden with seats for 250 patrons.

FOODIES FESTIVAL
MAP PAGE 102
Inverleith Park. www.foodiesfestival.com.
Early August

Wielding a list of corporate
sponsors as long as a string of aged
garlic and an all-star line-up of
Michelin star-holding chefs and
MasterChef and Great British
Bake Off winners, this UK-touring
festival pitches up in sunny
Inverleith in early August for three
days of interactive cooking, masterclasses and over-consumption. Aside
from all the nosh, there are deckchairs in front of a live music stage with
a large sandpit in view to keep the youngsters contained.

GRASSMARKET MARKET
MAP PAGE 56
Central Reservation, Grassmarket. www.stockbridgemarket.com/grassmarket.html. Sat
10am–5pm
Thriving little market with predominately artisan food sellers offering
the likes of freshly baked bread, cheese, olives and fresh veg as well as
delicious cooked meals such as paella.

LEITH MARKET
MAP PAGE 108
Dock Place, Leith. www.stockbridgemarket.com/leith.html. Sat 10am–4pm
Another satellite of Stockbridge Market, with a similar line-up of
fairtrade, organic and ethnic eats. Perfect for an after-market pint in the
beer garden at nearby *Teuchters Landing* (see page 113).

THE PITT
30 West Shore Rd, Granton. www.thepitt.co.uk/granton. Check website for details.
The pioneering street-food market is moving from Leith to an
independent venue space in Granton, with plans to open five days a
week and host foodie events, markets and pop-ups. The 2023 opening
date was delayed, with talk of 2024 as a more realistic timeframe.

STOCKBRIDGE MARKET
MAP PAGE 102
Kerr St, Stockbridge. www.stockbridgemarket.com. Sun 10am–4pm
Even with the belligerent Scottish climate, there's somehow an
international buzz as scores of locals and tourists dine out on paella or
Bombay street food, or wash a cupcake down with a coffee served out of
the back of a VW camper.

TUPINIQUIM
MAP PAGE 56
Top of Middle Meadow Walk, Lauriston Place, Old Town. www.tupiniquim.co.uk. Tues–Fri
noon–6pm, Sat until 7pm, Sun until 5pm
Edinburgh's best-loved food kiosk with dining garden to the rear,
this old police box turned funky Brazilian creperie has many a loyal
lunchtime customer. The legendary, gluten-free crepes come in both
sweet and savoury varieties, filled with everything from steak to
pumpkin to guava jam.

Edinburgh at a glance

Stockbridge p.100.
Moneyed Stockbridge remains one of Edinburgh's most distinctive suburbs, lined with singular shops, bars and bistros and bisected by the Water of Leith; adjacent Inverleith is home to the Royal Botanic Garden.

West End and Dean Village p.94.
Equal parts business and pleasure, Edinburgh's traffic-clogged West End is home to much of its financial sector as well as many of its theatres, concert halls and cinemas.

West Edinburgh p.114.
Leafy suburbs and prime addresses fan out from the western fringes of the New Town to rugby mecca Murrayfield and beyond.

South Edinburgh p.122.
The cosmopolitan suburbs of south Edinburgh range from the student heartland of Newington to the middle-class bustle of Bruntsfield and contentedly sedate Morningside.

Water of Leith

CANONMILLS

The Yard

EYRE PLACE

George V Park

DUNDAS STREET

DRUMMOND

STOCKBRIDGE

GREAT KING STREET

PLACE S

NORTHUMBERLAND STREET

NEW TOWN

Scottish National
Portrait Gallery

DEAN VILLAGE

Queen Street Gardens

QUEEN STREET

HANOVER STREET

St Andrew
& St George

QUEENSFERRY ROAD

Water of Leith

FREDERICK STREET

Assembly
Rooms

GEORGE STREET

CHARLOTTE SQUARE

West Register
House

ROSE STREET

PRINCES STREET

Royal
Scottish
Academy

WEST END

PRINCES STREET

National Gallery
of Scotland

WEST END

West Princes
Street Gardens

St Mary's
Cathedral

*WEST END-
PRINCES
STREET*

THEATRE
DISTRICT

LOTHIAN ROAD

Assembly Hall

The Hub

Edinburgh Castle

GRASSMARKET

WEST APPROACH ROAD

Edinburgh
Conference
Centre

HAYMARKET

George
Heriot's
School

LAURISTON PLACE

FOUNTAIN-
BRIDGE

MELVILLE DRIVE

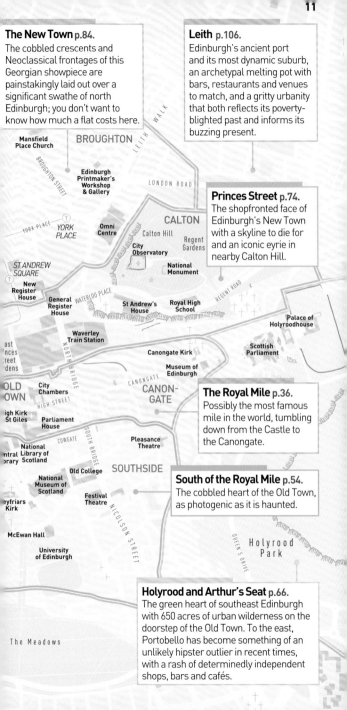

The New Town p.84.
The cobbled crescents and Neoclassical frontages of this Georgian showpiece are painstakingly laid out over a significant swathe of north Edinburgh; you don't want to know how much a flat costs here.

Leith p.106.
Edinburgh's ancient port and its most dynamic suburb, an archetypal melting pot with bars, restaurants and venues to match, and a gritty urbanity that both reflects its poverty-blighted past and informs its buzzing present.

Princes Street p.74.
The shopfronted face of Edinburgh's New Town with a skyline to die for and an iconic eyrie in nearby Calton Hill.

The Royal Mile p.36.
Possibly the most famous mile in the world, tumbling down from the Castle to the Canongate.

South of the Royal Mile p.54.
The cobbled heart of the Old Town, as photogenic as it is haunted.

Holyrood and Arthur's Seat p.66.
The green heart of southeast Edinburgh with 650 acres of urban wilderness on the doorstep of the Old Town. To the east, Portobello has become something of an unlikely hipster outlier in recent times, with a rash of determinedly independent shops, bars and cafés.

Mansfield Place Church
BROUGHTON
LEITH WALK
BROUGHTON STREET
Edinburgh Printmaker's Workshop & Gallery
LONDON ROAD
YORK PLACE
YORK PLACE
Omni Centre
CALTON
Calton Hill
Regent Gardens
City Observatory
National Monument
ST ANDREW SQUARE
New Register House
General Register House
WATERLOO PLACE
St Andrew's House
Royal High School
REGENT ROAD
Palace of Holyroodhouse
ast nces reet dens
Waverley Train Station
NORTH BRIDGE
Canongate Kirk
Museum of Edinburgh
Scottish Parliament
OLD OWN
City Chambers
HIGH STREET
CANONGATE
CANON-GATE
igh Kirk St Giles
Parliament House
SOUTH BRIDGE
COWGATE
Pleasance Theatre
National ntral Library of orary Scotland
Old College
SOUTHSIDE
National Museum of Scotland
Festival Theatre
eyfriars Kirk
NICOLSON STREET
McEwan Hall
University of Edinburgh
QUEEN'S DRIVE
Holyrood Park
The Meadows

15

Things not to miss

It's not possible to see everything that Edinburgh has to offer in one trip – and we don't suggest you try. What follows is a selective taste of the city's highlights, from its world-famous architecture to its August arts festivities.

> The Palace of Holyrood House
See page 66
For centuries the sometime residence of Scotland's royalty, with a hauntingly ruinous abbey.

< Edinburgh Castle
See page 36
One of the most iconic castles in the world, home to a celebrated military parade.

∨ The Scottish Parliament
See page 68
An architectural one-off that still divides opinion; squeeze in among the tourist hordes and decide for yourself.

< **Holyrood Park**
See page 70
Venture off the beaten track without leaving the city centre.

∨ **Hogmanay**
See page 152
The most popular New Year blowout on the planet; fireworks, ceilidhs and concerts into the wee small hours.

< Dr Neil's Garden

See page 71

Escape the tourist trail at this low-key idyll by Duddingston Village.

∨ The Old Town

See page 54

The haunted heart of old Edinburgh, with tenements, closes and catacombs piled up cheek-by-jowl.

∧ City skyline
See page 80
The jagged sightline southwest from Calton Hill, taking in the Old Town in all its brooding magnificence.

< Rosslyn Chapel
See page 132
Da Vinci Code fever may have cooled but this Gothic masterpiece is as mesmerizing as ever.

∧ Edinburgh's festivals
See page 26
Scotland's capital is home to the mother of all arts extravaganzas each August, but this is just one of the incredible festivals that the city stages annually.

∨ The New Town
See page 84
The Old Town's polar opposite, with dazzling Georgian crescents, postcard-pretty mews and manicured gardens.

∧ **The Shore**
See page 112
Leith's medieval port and surrounds are an epicurean enclave of Michelin stars, foraged produce and diverse eats.

< **Royal Botanic Garden**
See page 102
Edinburgh's showpiece gardens, with the world's biggest collection of wild Asian plants outside China.

< **Edinburgh Zoo**
See page 114
Roll up to see a veritable bounty of
furry, feathery and scaly creatures
at one of Europe's great zoos.

∨ **Edinburgh's pubs**
See page 7
From Scotland's oldest pub to
craft beer emporia to artisan gin
palaces, Edinburgh is a drinker's
paradise.

THINGS NOT TO MISS

Day One

The Scottish Parliament. See page 68. Get close up with Scotland's most talked-about building and – if the Parliament is in session – witness devolved government in action.

Palace of Holyroodhouse. See page 66. The former home of Scotland's Stewart kings and queens, with an atmospheric abbey ruin out back.

The Royal Mile. See page 36. Stroll for one full Scots mile along a thoroughfare Daniel Defoe described as "the largest, longest and finest...in the world".

Victoria Street. See page 54. Duck down this picturesque thoroughfare, lined with arcaded boutiques and flanked by a vertigo-inducing pedestrian walkway.

Lunch. See page 49. Drop into the dazzling *Signet Library* on the Royal Mile's Parliament Square for the most well-appointed of lunches.

Edinburgh Castle. See page 36. Castles don't come much more legendary than Edinburgh's – or as formidable; even Bonnie Prince Charlie couldn't breach it.

National Museum of Scotland. See page 59. All the Scottish heritage you could want, from stone Celtic crosses to the gruesome Millennium Clock Tower and idiosyncratic Lewis chessmen..

The Grassmarket. See page 54. Wind your way down Candlemaker Row to the historic Grassmarket, once a cattle mart, now a cobbled outdoor drinking spot, perfect for an aperitif.

Dinner. See page 62. Queue up for some tantalizing Thai treats at *Ting Thai Caravan*, Edinburgh's number one street-food destination.

Scottish Parliament

At Holyroodhouse

Princes Street Gardens

Day Two

The New Town. See page 84. Marvel at the Neoclassical neatness of Edinburgh's eighteenth-century showpiece and lose yourself amid its cobbled mews, gardens and terraces.

Scottish National Portrait Gallery. See page 86. The story of Scotland in famous physiognomy, with tens of thousands of portraits housed in a dramatic Gothic Revival pile.

Calton Hill. See page 80. The best vantage point in the city according to Robert Louis Stevenson, and he knew a good view when he saw one.

Lunch. See page 82. Pop round the back of Calton hill's Collective to *The Lookout by Gardener's Cottage* to feast on great food served with the finest views in town.

Princes Street Gardens. See page 77. Wander among squirrels, flowerbeds and mature trees in the magnificent shadow of the Edinburgh skyline.

National Gallery of Scotland. See page 79. Drop into Scotland's premier destination for pre-twentieth-century art.

West End Village. See page 94. Explore the boutiques, bistros and artisan cafés of this interminably affluent enclave.

Dinner. See page 98. Lower your carbon footprint at *Forage & Chatter*, a city culinary highlight, with ingredients sourced from within a 25-mile radius.

Royal Lyceum Theatre. See page 99. Don your finest to take in a show at this endearing Victorian hall.

Classic Edinburgh New Town streets

Dynamic Earth

Boutiques in Bruntsfield

Day Three

Scottish National Gallery of Modern Art. See page 97. Britain's first gallery dedicated to twentieth-century painting and sculpture, with a strong showing by the Scottish Colourists and a career's worth of genius by Leith's own Pop Art godfather, Eduardo Paolozzi.

Dean Village. See page 96. It's a bit of a hike out past the West End but this chocolate box-pretty village has an atmosphere all of its own.

Royal Botanic Garden. See page 102. Seventy acres of gorgeous green space, famous for its horticultural chinoiserie and handsome glasshouses.

Stockbridge. See page 100. Explore the cafés, bars and shops of this singular and perennially hip New Town satellite.

Lunch. See page 105. Seek out the quaint backstreet pub, *Kays bar* – a true Victorian delight hidden among the townhouses and mews cottages – and fill up on real ale and stovies.

Water of Leith. See page 101. Tackle as much or as little of the 13-mile Water of Leith walkway and keep your eyes peeled for herons, otters, dippers and even one of Antony Gormley's *Standing Man* statues.

Leith. See page 106. Take in the salty air at the Shore, Leith's quaint old harbour area, a melting pot of Michelin-starred restaurants, hipster foodie ventures and reclaimed arts hubs.

Dinner. See page 111. Get Michelin starstruck at celebrity chef Tom Kitchin's culinary stronghold, *The Kitchin*, one of Edinburgh's finest restaurants.

In the Royal Botanic Garden

Scottish National Gallery of Modern Art

Artisan food shop in Stockbridge

Green Edinburgh

Even the most full-on city break needs some downtime; recover your calm among Edinburgh's glorious green acres.

Holyrood Park. See page 70. A wonderland of an urban refuge, with no less than 650 acres of hills, glens, lochs and trails.

Arthur's Seat. See page 70. You can't visit Edinburgh without climbing this iconic volcano; just don't expect any knights or round tables.

Dr Neil's Garden. See page 71. An urban refuge within an urban refuge; feel the stress melting away as you sink onto a stone bench overlooking Duddingston Loch.

🍴 **Lunch.** See page 73. Follow in the footsteps of Stewart – *and* Hanoverian – royalty at Scotland's oldest pub, *The Sheep Heid*.

Meadows. See page 123. Wander the tree-lined walkways of this iconic park and – if it's sunny – picnic with the locals.

Blackford Hill. See page 124. A gentler climb than Arthur's Seat, and home to the Royal Observatory.

Hermitage of Braid. See page 124. Head straight from Blackford Hill into this ancient woodland-designated nature reserve, home to some of the city's most venerable old trees.

Pentland Hills. See page 133. If you have any energy left, take a bus out to the Pentland Hills for a bracing taste of rural Scottish upland.

🍴 **Dinner.** See page 127. Gird yourself for drinks and dinner in the living museum that is *The Canny Man's in* Morningside.

Arthur's Seat

Duddingston Loch's locals

Blackford Hill

Infamous Edinburgh

Dastardly deeds, gruesome exhibits, ghosts with a chip on their ectoplasmic shoulder – you'll find it all in the world's most haunted city.

James V's Tower, Palace of Holyroodhouse. See page 66. Scene of the murder of Mary, Queen of Scots' secretary, David Rizzio, with the blood stains supposedly still visible.

Surgeons' Hall Museum. See page 59. A conspicuously ostentatious exterior conceals one of Scotland's grisliest museum collections.

The Real Mary King's Close. See page 43. Dodge the ghosts in this dank warren of subterranean tenements, where plague victims were once entombed alive.

Lunch. See page 50. If your appetite hasn't deserted you, head to *Deacon's House Café*, set in the haunted close where the man who infamously inspired *Dr Jekyll and Mr Hyde* (see page 42) once lived.

South Bridge Vaults. See page 52. Home to a particularly unpleasant poltergeist, these notoriously creepy catacombs consistently take the honours as Edinburgh's most haunted.

Edinburgh Castle. See page 36. The Witches Well, or Fountain, marks the site where hundreds of women were burnt at the stake; some of whom are reported to stalk the Castle corridors.

Dinner. See page 51. Where else to dine after a hard day's ghost hunting but amid the Gothic splendour of *The Witchery by the Castle*.

Greyfriars Kirkyard. See page 56. Run the gauntlet of the downright dangerous McKenzie Poltergeist on a night-time tour into the depths of the Covenanter's Prison and Black Mausoleum.

Surgeons' Hall Museum

Deacon's House Café

Greyfriars Kirkyard

Budget Edinburgh

If you're watching your bank balance, it's entirely possible to enjoy an absorbing day's sightseeing completely free, and eat for a fraction of the typically prohibitive price.

Old Calton Burial Ground. See page 80. An atmospheric tangle of stones nevertheless, and abiding home to many of Edinburgh's great and good, including David Hume.

Scottish Poetry Library. See page 48. Everyone knows Rabbie Burns but here you'll discover a whole universe of native verse, including recordings in both Scots and Gaelic.

Museum of Childhood. See page 44. Expect nostalgia overdrive as you explore three floors of trains, games, dolls and hobbies for auld lang syne.

Museum of Edinburgh. See page 48. If you've been on the white-knuckle ghost tour of Greyfriars Kirkyard (see page 24), you might want to fill in some background in this maze of wood-panelled rooms, one of which displays the original National Covenant.

Lunch. See page 75. For cheap-as-chips eats, walk to the new Edinburgh Street Food by the OMNi Centre.

Old College and Talbot Rice Gallery. See page 59. Head south to the Robert Adam/William Playfair-designed Old College for an eyeful of contemporary and nineteenth-century art.

General Register House. See page 74. Pore over thousands of records dating back 500 years.

St Mary's Cathedral. See page 94. Catch the daily evensong and get spiritual beneath the glorious gothic arches.

Dinner. See page 91. Head back into town for some great-value hand-pressed tacos and antojitos at *El Cartel Mexicano.*

Scottish Poetry Library

Try a street food lunch

Dean Village

EDINBURGH'S FESTIVALS

The city of Edinburgh plays host to some of the world's most famous cultural festivals, many of them in sync in August each year (see page 30). In 1946, Scotland's historic capital was first proposed as the ultimate venue for a post-war "international festival", and nearly eight decades later, Edinburgh's citizens are joined by artists and audiences from every corner of the globe in celebration of culture and creativity. Music, comedy, theatre, dance, science and storytelling are all honoured at these much-loved events that take place around the year, staged in eclectic venues across the city.

Edinburgh Jazz and Blues Festival

Second two weeks in July
edinburghjazzfestival.com

One of the largest festivals of its kind in Europe, the Edinburgh Jazz & Blues Festival dates back to 1978 and has played host to some of the biggest names on the scene, from contemporary stars like Nubya Garcia and Ibibio Sound Machine to legends of the music, like BB King. Covering a huge range of

Edinburgh Jazz and Blues Festival

genres and spanning the entire history of the music from ragtime to modern jazz to Chicago blues and beyond, the festival is also a huge supporter of homegrown talent, with Scottish musicians forming the beating heart of the programme. As well as paid concerts, the festival's packed schedule includes two free events: the Mardi Gras, held in the Grassmarket on the festival's opening Saturday, and the Edinburgh Festival Carnival, Edinburgh's largest multicultural celebration. Gigs are held across the city, including at Festival Theatre, George Square and the intimate surroundings of *The Jazz Bar* (see page 65). Tickets generally £10–25.

The Royal Edinburgh Military Tattoo

Early to late August edintattoo.co.uk

The Royal Edinburgh Military Tattoo is a world-class event, rooted in Scottish tradition and offering audiences an experience like no other. Its vision is to be the world's greatest immersive event, producing atmospheric spectaculars that enrich lives through creativity, connection, and contribution. Held on the iconic Edinburgh Castle Esplanade, the Tattoo features music, precision performances and dance from military and cultural acts from around the globe – over 50 countries have been represented since its first show in 1950. Set against the stunning backdrop of Edinburgh Castle, all lit up with special projections, around 800 performers take to the stage across 25 performances throughout August, with a combined live audience of 220,000 each year.

Edinburgh International Festival

Early to late August eif.co.uk

Edinburgh International Festival, sometimes called the "Official Festival", is a celebration of world-class performing arts. Set up after World War II, the Festival platforms internationalism and cultural diversity. Traditionally a highbrow event offering opera, theatre, dance and classical music, the Festival has widened its horizons in recent years, with large-scale free events and contemporary music line-ups, including the likes of PJ Harvey and Mogwai. Performances take place at larger venues such as Usher Hall and the Festival Theatre; to meet artists and musicians, head to the home of the Festival, The Hub, at the top of the Royal Mile.

The Royal Edinburgh Military Tattoo

Edinburgh International Children's Festival

Healing a fractured world

Edinburgh's birth as a world festival city was originally seen as a means to heal the wounds of World War II. Formed in the shadow of that worldwide cataclysm, the first festivals sought to use culture as a healing balm to bring peoples and nations together in celebration of a common humanity and help 'the flowering of the human spirit'. Following the recent worldwide pandemic, and in the face of numerous global issues, this founding mantra is as relevant as ever and continues to inspire much of the annual festival programmes.

Edinburgh Festivals and Festival Venues

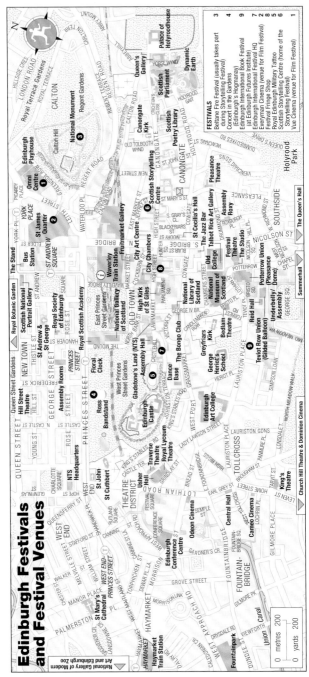

FESTIVALS

Beltane Fire Festival (usually takes part during Storytelling Festival)	3
Concert in the Gardens	4
Edinburgh's Hogmanay (Edinburgh's Hogmanay)	9
Edinburgh International Book Festival	2
Edinburgh Futures Institute (at Edinburgh Futures Institute)	7
Edinburgh International Festival HQ	8
Everyman Cinema (venue for Film Festival)	5
Festival Fringe Shop	6
Royal Edinburgh Military Tattoo	
Scottish Storytelling Centre (home of the Storytelling Festival)	
Vue Cinema (venue for Film Festival)	1

Edinburgh Festival Fringe

Early to late August edfringe.com

The Edinburgh Festival Fringe is one of the greatest celebrations of arts and culture on the planet. For three weeks in August, Scotland's capital welcomes an explosion of creative energy from around the globe. Artists and performers take to hundreds of stages all over the city to present shows for every taste. From big names in the world of entertainment to unknown artists looking to build their careers, the festival caters for everyone and includes theatre, comedy, dance, physical theatre, circus, cabaret, children's shows, musicals, opera, music, spoken word, exhibitions and events. Venues are as imaginative as the shows themselves: play-parks, restaurants and even parked cars have all been used to stage performances. Tickets (sold online, at venues or at the Fringe Box Office – Old Assembly Close, High Street, EH1 1QS) range from free to around £35, and it's always worth asking about deals at the box office's Half Price Hut. The Fringe street events – also free – are one of the world's leading displays of street performance.

Edinburgh Art Festival

August edinburghartfestival.com

Each August, the UK's largest annual festival of visual art presents high-profile exhibitions, performances, screenings and discussions from renowned artists such as Tracey Emin, Grayson Perry, Douglas Gordon and Ron Mueck, alongside some of the best emerging talent. Leading galleries and museums across the city participate, presenting exciting new commissions, exhibitions and events throughout the month. The majority of the programme is free

Edinburgh International Book Festival

to attend, with "pay what you can" options often available.

Edinburgh International Book Festival

Last two weeks of August edbookfest.co.uk

The Edinburgh International Book Festival is a celebration of the written (and spoken) word, featuring participants from across the globe and closer to home. The Book Festival is held in the heart of the city with a diverse, imaginative,

Edinburgh Science Festival

August in Edinburgh

Edinburgh really is a festival city, particularly in August when there's an electric atmosphere and visitors from across the globe. When people say "Edinburgh Festival", they don't usually realise there's more than one but instead a mash-up of festivals, including the International, the Fringe, the Military Tattoo, and the art, book and film festivals. The dynamism, spontaneity and sheer exuberance of the festivals dominate the city, with the headlining names going a long way to reinforce the city's cultural credibility.

There's something on every corner, in every conceivable type of venue (museums, bars, barges and public toilets have all played host to Edinburgh events), which provides an element of surprise and discovery for festival-goers. Pop-up preview performances are scheduled to give you a taste of the full-length show, and along the partly-pedestrianised Royal Mile (see page 36) you'll find even more street performers, portrait artists, living statues and balloonists than usual, plus all the usual people-watching spots from outdoor tables spilling out from cafes and bars. The famous main street runs through the heart of the Old Town from the castle to Holyrood Palace, and in August its entire length – and its closes (alleyways) and courtyards – is loud, colourful and fun, whatever the time of day (street performers tend to wrap up around 9pm, though festival performances are staged around the clock).

The mild, long days (the high latitude means the sun doesn't set until after 9pm) make August a great choice for a visit, and the other joy is that of course you're not just limited to festival events – all of Edinburgh's usual summer fun is at hand. Visit markets and fairs, like Saturday's Farmers Market on Castle Terrace or Leith Market on Dock Place, or Sunday's Stockbridge

Market on Saunders Street; explore the Royal Botanic Garden (see page 102); climb Calton Hill (see page 80) or Arthur's Seat (see page 70); or follow the Water of Leith walkway (see page 101) through Dean and Stockbridge towards Leith (see page 106). The city's parks are wonderful green spaces to enjoy a relaxed festival moment: take a picnic to Princes Street Gardens, Holyrood Park, Dunbar's Close, Scotland Yard Park or Inverleith Park. And if the weather is being really kind, then Portobello ("Porty") Beach beckons for a dip.

All this peak August festivals fun does mean you must book accommodation well ahead of time, and expect to pay more than at other times of the year. Don't forget that Edinburgh is a relatively compact city and easy to walk around on foot, even to further-afield residential neighbourhoods like Newington, Bruntsfield and Morningside, so you don't necessarily have to stretch to Old Town prices (some people even stay in Glasgow and take the train). Student halls are a great choice if you can nab them (see universityrooms.com).

It can be a little overwhelming deciding what events to book – keep an eye on official websites and on social media for announcements and predictions about what not to miss. Big name events, including the Military Tattoo, may well sell out in advance so you'll have to be quick to snap up tickets. The Fringe is an open-access event, meaning that any artist or performer can participate: returning acts or those at the major venues are considered a safe bet. Remember that there are thousands of shows with tickets available each day some of them operating under "£10 on the day", "half price" or "pay what you want". And there's all the free (donations appreciated) street performances. Wear comfy shoes, expect crowds, shake off your FOMO (fear of missing out) and embrace the joy of discovery.

Scottish International Storytelling Festival

and inclusive programme. There is something for everyone, no matter your age – with talks, readings, and signings by visiting authors, panel discussions, and workshops. Join well-known Scottish authors, Booker Prize winners, as well as the odd rock star, head of state or actor on site. Ticket prices are varied, with many free and "pay what you can" events.

Edinburgh's Hogmanay

Edinburgh International Film Festival

Mid-August edfilmfest.org.uk

Established in 1947, this festival runs as an annual celebration of cinema, at the heart of the Scottish capital's summer festival season. Centering film as a major art form within a vibrant, creative conversation, EIFF presents welcoming public screenings of new feature films, retrospectives and short films, mixing fiction, documentaries, animation and films by artists. Renowned for its innovative programming and talent-spotting, the festival nurtures exceptional homegrown and international talent, with filmmakers who have presented early films at EIFF including Martin Scorsese, Claire Denis, George Lucas, Jane Campion, David Cronenberg and many more. The Festival also facilitates training schemes and acts as a crucial meeting place for filmmakers and industry professionals to connect. Expect to discover your new favourite movie, and possibly meet the filmmaker in the bar afterwards.

Edinburgh's Hogmanay

Four days around New Year's Eve edinburghshogmanay.com

Hogmanay is Scotland's traditional celebration of the New Year, an event the country embraces with raucous celebration, ancient traditions and more than a few whiskies. And nowhere does it quite like Edinburgh. The four-day festival launches with the Torchlight Procession (29 December), where 20,000 people create a river of fire with flaming torches through the historic Old Town. A massive Street Party, held on Princes Street on 31st December, welcomes friends from around the world, united in celebration and anticipation for the explosive Midnight Fireworks from

Edinburgh Castle. Over 50,000 attend events on NYE, which also includes the Concert in the Gardens featuring A-list pop, rock and indie bands, and an outdoor ceilidh with traditional Scottish music and dancing. Edinburgh's Hogmanay has grown from a 90's drunken, stranger-snogging celebration of the midnight bells, to an eclectic array of cultural events over four days, including free live music across the city for First Footin', and an afternoon of events for children and families on 1st January called Sprogmanay. Tickets for all official events are available online, but the Street Party and concert sell-out in advance.

Great festivals in the rest of the year

EDINBURGH SCIENCE FESTIVAL
Two weeks around Easter time sciencefestival.co.uk

The Science Festival has inspiring and interactive events, immersive art and exhibitions for all ages, from hands-on workshops and shows for children to discussions and science themed nights out for adults. Bringing together the brightest minds from around the globe, Edinburgh Science Festival leads the world in delivering live science experiences – taking science out of the lab for all to enjoy. Venues include National Museum of Scotland, Dynamic Earth, Summerhall, Royal Botanic Garden Edinburgh and City Art Centre. Some events free; some ticketed (£5–20).

EDINBURGH INTERNATIONAL CHILDREN'S FESTIVAL
May/June imaginate.org.uk/festival

The Edinburgh International Children's Festival is a celebration of performing arts for children and young people, presenting an annual programme of international theatre, circus, puppetry and dance for ten days at the end of May. Its international programme goes way beyond expectations of children's work, addressing important themes and pushing boundaries with performances that are deeply engaging, innovative and inspiring. Many of the shows are visually striking, often very humorous and will appeal to children as well as adults, so if you're lucky enough to be in Edinburgh at that time of year, it's worth a visit. The Festival opens with a free family day. Tickets for all other shows are around £9.

SCOTTISH INTERNATIONAL STORYTELLING FESTIVAL
Mid-late October sisf.org.uk

The Scottish International Storytelling Festival is the world's largest celebration of storytelling, anchored in Scotland, a nation of storytellers. It takes place in October each year, as the seasons change with long nights drawing families and friends around the hearth, inspired by the Scottish ceilidh tradition – a community gathering full of tales, anecdotes, music and song. Expert storytellers command the attention of the room as they weave their tales of life, love, magic and mystery, with audience involvement being a key component of the festival. From the Scottish Storytelling Centre, the festival's main hub located on the Royal Mile, the festival spreads out across Scotland, offering live performances, workshops, story walks and events in family-friendly outdoor spaces. Tickets £6–15 (some free events). Check ahead to see if an event is suitable for children.

PLACES

Royal Mile

The Royal Mile

The Royal Mile's tight, foreboding closes dwarfed by soaring rubble-stone merchant houses and grand neo-Grecian sandstone buildings make it a veritable feast of architectural heritage. Scratch the surface and it gets even more interesting: many of the structures conceal a medieval subterranean world of caverns, rooms and closes, some of which can be visited on tours while others are yet to be rediscovered. The Royal Mile spans four separate streets in one, long row – Castlehill, Lawnmarket, High Street, Canongate – bookended by the Castle and the Palace of Holyroodhouse. In between, you'll discover an enviable number of sights and attractions, only exceeded (and somewhat detracted) by the inexhaustible knitwear, tartan and shortbread outlets that, along with the ever-present bagpiper, draw tourists here in their droves.

Edinburgh Castle

MAP PAGE 37
Castlehill. www.edinburghcastle.scot.
Charge; HES.

The history of Edinburgh is tightly wrapped up with its **Castle**, which dominates the city from a lofty seat atop an extinct volcanic rock. It requires no great imaginative feat to comprehend the strategic importance that underpinned the Castle's, and hence Edinburgh's, pre-eminence in Scotland. From Princes Street, the north side rears high

Edinburgh Castle

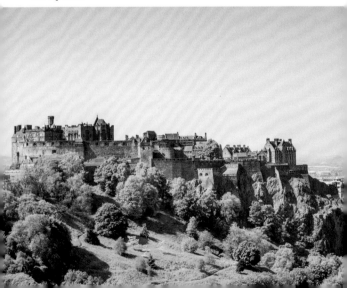

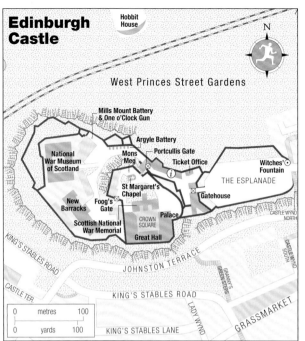

Edinburgh Castle

Hobbit House

West Princes Street Gardens

N

Mills Mount Battery & One o'Clock Gun

Argyle Battery

Portcullis Gate

National War Museum of Scotland

Mons Meg

Ticket Office

Witches' Fountain

THE ESPLANADE

St Margaret's Chapel

New Barracks

Foog's Gate

Gatehouse

CASTLE WYND NORTH

Scottish National War Memorial

CROWN SQUARE

Palace

Great Hall

CASTLE WYND SOUTH

KING'S STABLES ROAD

JOHNSTON TERRACE

GRANNY'S GREEN STEPS

CASTLE TER.

KING'S STABLES ROAD

LADY WYND

GRASSMARKET

0 metres 100

0 yards 100

KING'S STABLES LANE

above an almost sheer rock face; the southern side is equally formidable and the western, where the rock rises in terraces, only marginally less so. Would-be attackers, like modern tourists, were forced to approach the Castle from the narrow ridge to the east – today's Royal Mile. The disparate styles of the fortifications reflect the change in its role from defensive citadel to national monument, and today, as well as attracting more paying visitors than any other sight in Scotland, the Castle is still a military barracks and home to the **Honours of Scotland**, the nation's crown jewels.

The Esplanade to Mill's Mount

MAP PAGE 37

The Castle is entered via the **Esplanade**, a parade ground laid out in the eighteenth century and enclosed by ornamental walls. In the summer huge grandstands are

erected for the Edinburgh Military Tattoo (see page 26), which takes place nightly during the Edinburgh Festival. A shameless and spectacular pageant of swinging kilts and massed pipe bands, the tattoo makes full use of its dramatic setting. Various memorials are dotted around the Esplanade, including the pretty Art Nouveau **Witches' Fountain** commemorating the three hundred or more women burnt at this spot on charges of sorcery, the last of whom died in 1722.

Edinburgh Castle has a single entrance, a 10ft-wide opening in the **gatehouse**, one of many Romantic-style additions made in the 1880s, through which you'll find the main ticket office on your right. Continue uphill, showing your ticket as you pass through the handsome sixteenth-century **Portcullis Gate,** and you'll soon arrive at the eighteenth-century,

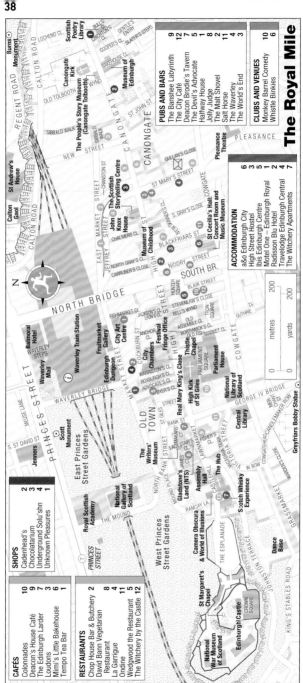

The Royal Mile

CAFÉS

Colonnades	10
Deacon's House Café	9
The Edinburgh Larder	7
Loudons	3
Mimi's Little Bakehouse	6
Tempo Tea Bar	1

RESTAURANTS

Chop House Bar & Butchery	2
David Bann Vegetarian Restaurant	8
La Garrigue	4
Ondine	11
Wedgwood the Restaurant	5
The Witchery by the Castle	12

SHOPS

Cadenhead's	2
Chocolatarium	3
Underground Solu'shn	4
Unknown Pleasures	1

PUBS AND BARS

The Banshee Labyrinth	9
The City Café	12
Deacon Brodie's Tavern	7
The Devil's Advocate	5
Halfway House	1
Jolly Judge	8
The Malt Shovel	2
Salt Horse	11
The Waverley	4
The World's End	3

CLUBS AND VENUES

Monkey Barrel Comedy	10
Whistle Binkies	6

ACCOMMODATION

a&o Edinburgh City	6
High Street Hostel	3
Ibis Edinburgh Centre	5
Motel One – Edinburgh Royal	1
Radisson Blu Hotel	2
Travelodge Edinburgh Central	4
The Witchery Apartments	7

Crown Square at Edinburgh Castle

six-gun **Argyle Battery**. A few further steps west on **Mill's Mount Battery**, a well-known Edinburgh ritual takes place – the daily firing of the **one o'clock gun**.

National War Museum of Scotland

MAP PAGE 37
Entry included in Castle ticket price.
Continuing on the main path past the Argyle Battery, look out for the **National War Museum of Scotland** on your right. Covering the past four hundred years of Scottish military history, the slant of the museum is towards the soldiers who fought for the Union, rather than against it. While the rooms are packed with uniforms, medals, paintings of heroic actions and plenty of interesting memorabilia, the museum manages to convey a reflective, human tone.

St Margaret's Chapel

MAP PAGE 37
Near the highest point of the citadel is tiny Romanesque **St Margaret's Chapel**, the oldest surviving building in the Castle, and probably in Edinburgh.

Although once believed to have been built by the saint herself and mooted as the site of her death in 1093, its architectural style suggests that it actually dates from about thirty years later. In front of the chapel, you'll see the famous fifteenth-century siege gun, **Mons Meg**, which could fire a 500lb stone nearly two miles.

Crown Square

MAP PAGE 37
The historic heart of the Castle, Crown Square is the most important and secure section of the entire complex. The eastern side is occupied by the **Palace**, a surprisingly unassuming edifice begun in the 1430s, which owes its Renaissance appearance to King James IV. There's access to a few rooms here including the tiny, panelled bedchamber where Mary, Queen of Scots gave birth to James VI.

The Palace also houses a detailed audio-visual presentation on the **Honours of Scotland**, a potent image of Scotland's nationhood; the originals are housed in the Crown Room at the very end of the display. The glass case containing the Honours has been rearranged to create space for the incongruously plain **Stone of Destiny**, a coronation throne on which all kings of Scotland were crowned from AD838 until Edward I stole it in 1296. The stone was returned ceremoniously from Westminster Abbey in 1996.

On the south side of Crown Square is James IV's hammer beam-ceilinged **Great Hall**, used for meetings of the Scottish Parliament until 1639.

Scotch Whisky Experience

MAP PAGE 38
354 Castlehill. www.scotchwhisky experience.co.uk. Charge for tours.

The **Scotch Whisky Experience** mimics the kind of tours offered at distilleries in the Highlands, and while it can't match the authenticity of the real thing, the centre does offer a thorough introduction to the "water of life" (*uisge beatha* in Gaelic). Tours feature an entertaining tutorial on the specialized art of whisky nosing, a gimmicky ride in a moving "barrel" car, a peek at the world's largest whisky collection

At the Camera Obscura

and a tasting. The Silver tour (50min) is the one to go for if you have a casual interest in the subject or are with children who get in half price (and taste 'Scotland's other national drink', Irn-Bru). For a deeper understanding of the drink consider a masterclass, which includes a sensory perception test followed by a comparative tasting featuring a blend, a grain and two single malt whiskies. On your way out, a well-stocked shop gives an idea of the sheer range and diversity of the drink, while downstairs there's a pleasant whisky bar and restaurant, *Amber* (see page 50), both of which can be visited without going on a tour. In 2023, a £3million revamp got underway at the Scotch Whisky Experience, with new tours apparently drawing on innovative tech not yet used in the whisky tourism world, though the exact details are being kept under wraps for now – watch this space.

Camera Obscura and World of Illusions

MAP PAGE 38
549 Castlehill. www.camera-obscura.co.uk. Charge, under-5s free.

Edinburgh's **Camera Obscura** has been a tourist attraction since 1853. Housed in the domed black-and-white turret on the roof, the "camera" consists of a small, darkened room with a white wooden table onto which a periscope reflects live images of prominent buildings and folk walking on the streets below. Today, the camera is greatly overshadowed by the **World of Illusions**, a labyrinth of family-friendly exhibits of optical illusions, holograms and clever visual trickery. Spread across the five floors below the camera, displays are playfully interactive, like the Maze of Mirrors or the Vortex where you attempt to walk across a static ramp surrounded by a rotating tunnel – much harder than you might think. There's also

The Writers' Museum

the Big-Small room where photos taken from the viewing window reveal giant children towering over their shrunken parents.

The Hub

MAP PAGE 38
348 Castlehill. www.thehub-edinburgh.com. Free.

The imposing black church at the foot of Castlehill is **The Hub**, also known as "Edinburgh's Festival Centre". It's open year-round, providing performance, rehearsal and exhibition space, a ticket centre and a café. The building itself was constructed in 1845 to designs by James Gillespie Graham and Augustus Pugin – one of the architects of the Houses of Parliament in London – a connection obvious from the superb neo-Gothic detailing and the sheer presence of the building, whose spire is the highest in Edinburgh.

Gladstone's Land

MAP PAGE 38
477b Lawnmarket. www.nts.org.uk. Charge; NTS.

Tall, narrow **Gladstone's Land** is the Royal Mile's best surviving example of a typical seventeenth-century tenement. The building would have been home to various families living in cramped conditions: the well-to-do Gledstanes, who built it in 1620, are thought to have occupied the third floor. The National Trust for Scotland has carefully restored the rooms, filling them with period furnishings and fittings. The arcaded and wooden-fronted ground floor is home to a reconstructed cloth shop; pass through this and you encounter a warren of tight little staircases, tiny rooms, creaking floorboards and peek-hole windows. The finest room, on the first floor immediately above the arcade, has a marvellous Renaissance painted ceiling that was only discovered in the 1930s after the building was saved from demolition. After a £1.5-million restoration, Gladstone's Land reopened in 2021 with new interactive displays designed to connect visitors with the people who once lived here. One floor, opening for the first time, has been reimagined as an early twentieth-century boarding house inspired by widow Mary

Wilson, who took out a newspaper advert in 1911 listing a room in her apartment as suitable lodgings for 'two or three respectable men'. A new ground-floor coffee shop and ice-cream parlour are rooted in the past; the latter offers flavours like elderflower and lemon curd, and a sundae called "The Butcher" – vanilla, whisky and bacon – in homage to a former resident.

Writers' Museum

MAP PAGE 38
Lady Stairs Close, Lawnmarket.
www.edinburghmuseums.org.uk. Free.

Situated within the seventeenth-century Lady Stair's House, the **Writers' Museum** is dedicated to Scotland's three greatest literary lions: Sir Walter Scott, Robert Louis Stevenson and Robert Burns. It's a small affair with displays of first-edition copies, original manuscripts and personal effects, including Burn's original writing desk; a pair of riding boots given to Stevenson by a Samoan chief, engraved with the word "Tusitala" meaning "storyteller"; and the original press used to print Scott's Waverley novels. The house's tight, winding stairs and poky, wood-panelled rooms offer an authentic and attractive flavour of the medieval Old Town.

Parliament Square

MAP PAGE 38
High St.

Named after Parliament House – the seventeenth-century building that was Scotland's political chamber prior to the 1707 Act of Union – **Parliament Square** is an impressive and unexpected opening beside the Royal Mile that contains the High Kirk of St Giles and the Mercat Cross – a small stone structure common in Scottish burghs that would be used to make Royal pronouncements and around which markets could be held. Beside the kirk, the pattern set in the cobblestones near the main entrance to St Giles is known as the

Deacon Brodie

As the real-life, late eighteenth-century inspiration for Robert Louis Stevenson's novel, *The Strange Case of Dr Jekyll and Mr Hyde*, Deacon Brodie saw no contradiction in flirting with the gutter while getting on with the day job. A highly respected councillor, master cabinet maker, locksmith and heir to his father's fortune during working hours and a drinking, gambling and womanizing debauchee after dark, Brodie was a regular in the seedy taverns of Edinburgh's darker closes.

Eventually, his bad habits caught up with him as the burden of his two mistresses, five illegitimate children and gambling debts spiralled out of control. As trusted locksmith for Edinburgh's gentry, the temptation to copy keys proved too much for him and he and his criminal cohorts began targeting their properties. The raids became ever more audacious until eventually an attempt to rob the excise house was disturbed and one of the gang lost his nerve and turned himself in. Knowing that the game was up, Brodie fled to Holland but was captured and returned home to face justice. Sentenced to hang on Lawnmarket, ironically on the very gallows that he himself had designed, Brodie had one last dodge up his sleeve: wearing a steel collar, he intended to survive the noose and escape. Records show he was unsuccessful, although subsequent 'sightings' of him in Paris enhanced his legend.

The Thistle Chapel at St Giles

Heart of Midlothian, a nickname for the Edinburgh Tolbooth, which stood on this spot and was regarded as the heart of the city. The prison attached to the Tolbooth was immortalized in Sir Walter Scott's novel *Heart of Midlothian*, and you may still see locals spitting on the cobblestone heart, a continuation of the tradition of spitting on the door of the prison to ward off the evil contained therein.

High Kirk of St Giles

MAP PAGE 38

High St. www.stgilescathedral.org.uk. Free.
The **High Kirk of St Giles** is the original parish church of medieval Edinburgh, from where John Knox (see page 45) launched and directed the Scottish Reformation. St Giles is often referred to as a cathedral, though it has only been the seat of a bishop on two brief and unhappy occasions in the seventeenth century. The resplendent **crown spire** of the kirk is formed from eight flying buttresses and dates back to 1485, while **inside**, the four massive piers supporting the tower were part of a Norman church built here around 1120. In the nineteenth century,

St Giles was adorned with a whole series of funerary monuments on the model of London's Westminster Abbey; around the same time, it acquired several attractive Pre-Raphaelite stained-glass windows designed by Edward Burne-Jones and William Morris.

Thistle Chapel

MAP PAGE 38

At the southeastern corner of St Giles, the **Thistle Chapel** was built by Sir Robert Lorimer in 1911 as the private chapel of the sixteen knights of the Most Noble Order of the Thistle, the highest chivalric order in Scotland. Based on St George's Chapel in Windsor, it's an exquisite piece of craftsmanship, with an elaborate ribbed vault, huge drooping bosses and extravagantly ornate stalls showing off Lorimer's bold Arts and Crafts styling.

The Real Mary King's Close

MAP PAGE 38

2 Warriston's Close, High St. www.realmary kingsclose.com. Charge.
When work on the Royal Exchange, known as the City Chambers, began in 1753, the existing tenements

that overlooked **Mary King's Close** were only partially demolished to make way for the new building being constructed on top of them. The process left large sections of the houses, together with the old closes that ran alongside them, intact but entirely enclosed within the basement and cellars of the City Chambers. You can visit this rather spooky subterranean "lost city" on **tours** led by costumed actors, who take you round the cold stone shells of the houses where various scenes from the Close's history have been recreated. As you'd expect, blood, plague, pestilence and ghostly apparitions are to the fore, though there is an acknowledgement of the more prosaic side of medieval life in the archaeological evidence of an urban cow byre. The tour ends with a stroll up the remarkably well-preserved close itself.

St Cecilia's Hall: Concert Room and Music Museum

MAP PAGE 38
50 Niddry St. www.ed.ac.uk/visit/museums-galleries/st-cecilias. Free.
An unexpected delight located down grimy Niddry Street,

Museum of Childhood

Edinburgh University's **Music Museum** contains an impressive acquirement of historical musical instruments from around the world, many of which are mesmerizingly beautiful like the nineteenth-century stringed Indian *mayuri* carved into a peacock. Upstairs, regular public recitals in Scotland's oldest purpose-built concert hall – from 1762 – are a unique and intimate affair. See the website for what's on.

Museum of Childhood

MAP PAGE 38
42 High St. www.edinburghmuseums.org.uk. Free.
Harking back to simpler times, the **Museum of Childhood** hosts a joyful collection of toys, clothes, dolls and bikes that kids used to cherish before the advent of plastic. Over the five small exhibition spaces, there's a surprisingly large amount to see here, including a beautiful model railway scene, a room dedicated to childhood hobbies and some fancy old Victorian dollhouses.

Scottish Storytelling Centre

MAP PAGE 38
43–45 High St. www.scottishstorytellingcentre.com. Free; charge for John Knox House.
There are two distinct parts to the **Scottish Storytelling Centre**. One half is a stylish contemporary development containing an excellent café, the Netherbow Theatre – which hosts regular performances, often aimed at a younger audience – and an airy **Storytelling Court** with a small permanent exhibition about Scottish stories from ancient folk tales to *Harry Potter*. By contrast, **John Knox House** next door – but part of the same complex – is a fifteenth-century stone-and-timber building which, with its distinctive external staircase, overhanging upper storeys and busy

John Knox

Protestant reformer **John Knox** has been credited with, or blamed for, the distinctive national characteristic of rather gloomy reserve that emerged from the Calvinist Reformation and which has cast its shadow right up to the present. Little is known about Knox's early years: he was born between 1505 and 1514 in East Lothian and trained for the priesthood at the University of St Andrews. Ordained in 1540, Knox then served as a private tutor, in league with Scotland's first significant Protestant leader, **George Wishart**. After Wishart was burnt at the stake for heresy in 1546, Knox became involved with the group who had carried out the revenge murder of the Scottish primate, Cardinal David Beaton.

When Mary Tudor, a Catholic, acceded to the English throne in 1553, Knox fled to the Continent to avoid becoming embroiled in the religious turmoil. Returning two years later, he took over as spiritual leader of the Reformation, becoming minister of St Giles in Edinburgh, where he gained a reputation as a charismatic preacher. The establishment of Protestantism as the official religion of Scotland in 1560 was dependent on the forging of an alliance with **Elizabeth I**, which Knox himself rigorously championed: the swift deployment of English troops against the French garrison in Edinburgh dealt a fatal blow to Franco–Spanish hopes of re-establishing Catholicism in both Scotland and England. Although the return of **Mary, Queen of Scots** the following year placed a Catholic monarch on the Scottish throne, Knox was reputedly always able to retain the upper hand in his famous disputes with her.

Before his death in 1572, Knox began sweeping away all vestiges of episcopal control of the **Scots Kirk** and giving lay people a role of unprecedented importance. He proposed a nationwide education system, compulsory for the very young and free for the poor. His final legacy was the posthumously published *History of the Reformation of Religion in the Realm of Scotland*, a justification of his life's work.

pantile roof, is a classic example of the Royal Mile in its medieval heyday. Inside, the house is all low doorways, uneven floors and ornate wooden panelling; it contains a series of displays about Knox, the minister who established Calvinist Presbyterianism as the dominant religious force in the country.

The People's Story Museum

MAP PAGE 38
Canongate Tolbooth, 163 Canongate. www.edinburghmuseums.org.uk. Free.
Dominated by a turreted steeple and an odd external box clock, the late sixteenth-century **Canongate Tolbooth** has served both as the headquarters of the burgh administration and as a prison. It now houses **The People's Story Museum**, which contains a series of display cases, dense information boards and rather old-fashioned tableaux dedicated to the everyday life and work of Edinburgh's population through the centuries. This isn't one of Edinburgh's essential museums, but it does have a down-to-earth reality often missing from places dedicated to high culture or famous historical characters.

Literary Edinburgh

While Edinburgh's fine skyline, world-renowned festivals, art galleries and architectural heritage draw in a mushrooming number of visitors every year, it is arguably literary tourism that is having the city's most impressive renaissance. A new generation of writers who, like the classic novelists of the past, have found inspiration among Edinburgh's ancient howfs (pub in Old Scots), tight closes and grand Georgian buildings, are enticing visitors to seek out specific tour companies that will escort them to their favourite book locations.

The **Harry Potter** tours are enduringly popular. Take a stroll down Victoria Street, the inspiration for **Diagon Alley** where there's now a dedicated Potter shop, **Diagon House** (see page 60), and then enter the Greyfriars Kirkyard to look for the final resting place of Thomas Riddell, AKA Lord Voldemort. Behind the wall is **George Heriot's School** (see page 55), which gave rise to the concept of Hogwarts School of Witchcraft and Wizardry. Another tombstone here displays the name William McGonagall, a probable name source for the Hogwarts Professor, played in the film adaption by Maggie Smith who coincidently acted out a scene in this very kirkyard as the star of Muriel Spark's ***The Prime of Miss Jean Brodie***.

Cult fiction novels have their fair share of pilgrims too. Irvine Welsh's ***Trainspotting*** film adaptions show off some of Edinburgh's more iconic cityscapes while also introducing some of its less savoury localities like Leith's notorious **Banana flats** (see page 107), used as Sick Boy's drug den.

The majority of Edinburgh's literary acclaim is reserved for Scotland's Romanticist authors, however. None more so than that of Sir Walter Scott, whose accolades include the main station (Waverley) and a football team (Heart of Midlothian),

both named after his novels, while the Scott Monument (see page 78) is the largest dedication to an author in the world. Naturally, his works also feature prominently in the Writers' Museum (see page 42) collection alongside those of Robert Louis Stevenson and national poet Robert Burns, who are both immortalized in statues around the city. Look out for Stevenson's *Kidnapped* bronze, featuring the story's two main protagonists on the edge of Corstorphine hill, sight of their final parting; conveniently for sightseers, also on the airport bus route.

Edinburgh's passion for

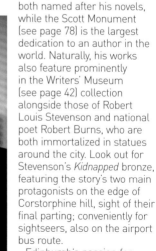

literature is not just inward looking. The relatively recent additions to the Royal Mile of the Scottish Storytelling Centre (see page 44) and the Scottish Poetry Library (see page 48) have widened the focus internationally and, together with the thriving Edinburgh International Book Festival (see page 29) in August, helped Edinburgh scoop the first UNESCO City of Literature designation in 2004.

Tours

EDINBURGH LITERARY PUB TOUR
Departs from outside the Beehive Inn, 18–20 Grassmarket. www.edinburghliterarypub tour.co.uk. Charge.

A pub crawl where you'll be introduced to the scenes, characters and words of the major figures of Scottish literature. Hosted by a pair of well-seasoned actors, tours offer the opportunity to procure a swift ale at each of the four pubs visited on the walk/crawl from the Grassmarket to Rose Street.

POTTER TRAIL
Departs from Greyfriars Bobby statue, Candlemaker Row. http://pottertrail.com. Free but donations welcomed. No booking required.

A muggle-friendly tour of all the Harry Potter sights. With wand in hand – given out at the start – you'll encounter the gravestones, cobbled lanes and ancient buildings that inspired the books while being thoroughly entertained by your enthusiastic wizard guide. Look out for the extended magic tours (see website for dates) where a local magician adds to the sorcery.

Canongate Kirk

Museum of Edinburgh

MAP PAGE 38

142–146 Canongate. www.edinburgh
museums.org.uk. Free.

Housing the city's principal
collection devoted to local history,
the **Museum of Edinburgh** is as
interesting for the labyrinthine
network of wood-panelled rooms
as it is for its rather quirky array of
artefacts. These do, however, include
a number of items of real historical
significance, in particular the
National Convention, the petition
for religious freedom drawn up on
a deerskin parchment in 1638, and
the original plans for the layout
of the New Town drawn by James
Craig chosen by the city council
after a competition in 1767.

Canongate Kirk

MAP PAGE 38

153 Canongate. www.canongatekirk.org.uk.
Free.

Built to house the congregation
expelled from Holyrood Abbey
when the latter was commandeered
by James VII (James II in England),
Canongate Kirk is the Royal
Family's church when they're at
Holyrood and was the location for
Britain's "other royal wedding" of
2011, when Prince William's cousin
Zara Phillips married England
rugby player Mike Tindall. The
kirk has a modesty rarely seen in
churches built in later centuries,
with a graceful curved facade and a
bow-shaped gable to the rear. The
surrounding churchyard provides
an attractive and tranquil stretch
of green in the heart of the Old
Town and affords fine views of
Calton Hill; it also happens to be
one of the city's most exclusive
cemeteries – well-known internees
include the political economist
Adam Smith, Mrs Agnes McLehose
(better known as Robert Burns's
"Clarinda") and Robert Fergusson,
regarded by some as Edinburgh's
greatest poet, despite his death
at the age of 24. Fergusson's
headstone was donated by Burns, a
fervent admirer, and a statue of the
young poet can be seen just outside
the kirk gates.

Scottish Poetry Library

MAP PAGE 38

5 Crichton's Close, Canongate.
www.scottishpoetrylibrary.org.uk. Free.

A small island of modern
architectural eloquence amid
a cacophony of large-scale
developments, the **Scottish
Poetry Library**'s attractive design
harmoniously combines brick, oak,
glass, Caithness stone and blue
ceramic tiles while incorporating a
section of an old city wall. Inside,
you'll encounter Scotland's most
comprehensive collection of native
poetry, and visitors are free to read
the books, periodicals and leaflets
found on the shelves, or listen to
recordings of poetry in the nation's
three tongues, Lowland Scots, Scots
Gaelic and English. The library's
main focus is on modern and post-
War Scottish poetry; however, with
over 45,000 items on the shelves
there's plenty of choice of historical
and international verse, particularly
European, many examples of which
have been translated into English.

Shops

Cadenhead's

MAP PAGE 38

172 Canongate. www.cadenhead.scot.

There's no end of opportunity to buy whisky in Edinburgh but this little business, dating back to the early Victorian era, is a must. While the range on offer can't match the scale of the larger operations further up the Royal Mile, quality beats quantity here with an expertly fine-tuned selection. As a bonus, there are always plenty samples on offer and no pressure or obligation to buy.

Chocolatarium

MAP PAGE 38

3–5 Cranston St. www.chocolatarium.co.uk.

Small chocolate museum that offers tours and tastings, and also has a shop selling artisan bars in flavour combinations you'd probably never have considered, and perhaps in the case of the camel milk chocolate, wouldn't want to.

Royal Mile Market

Underground Solu'shn

MAP PAGE 38

9 Cockburn St. www.underground solushn.com.

Edinburgh's last remaining record shop dedicated to dance and electronic music, with a huge selection of vinyl and CDs, plus some nice clothing and accessories. There's a row of decks so you can try before you buy.

Unknown Pleasures

MAP PAGE 38

110 Canongate. www.vinylnet.co.uk.

A surprise and relief to find a real shop on the Royal Mile that's not selling tartan or tablet. This secondhand vinyl and CD outlet has lots of rarities and classic albums to rummage through as well as a decent offering of posters and t-shirts.

Cafés

Colonnades

MAP PAGE 38

The Signet Library, Parliament Square. www.thesignetlibrary.co.uk.

Afternoon tea in the plushest of surroundings – and a giant gourmet leap above the standard egg-and-cress sandwiches. Here, it's coronation sweet potato and spinach, spiced cranberry Battenberg and, naturally, scones. Careful not to splutter your Earl Grey when the bill arrives: £60 per person. ££££

Deacon's House Café

MAP PAGE 38

Brodie's Close, 304 Lawnmarket. www.deaconshousecafe.co.uk.

Look out for the life-sized mannequin of Deacon Brodie (see page 42) at the entrance to this café's close. Both the period decor and pretty outside seating area, not to mention the light, crumbly scones, make it a welcome respite from the frenetic Royal Mile. £

The Edinburgh Larder

MAP PAGE 38

15 Blackfriars St. www.edinburgh larder.co.uk.

Overwhelmingly popular café-diner dishing up top-notch breakfast favourites like the Full

Scottish and the brioche eggy bread with cinnamon sugar and syrup. There are also gluten-free cakes, plus light lunches like soups, sandwiches and daily specials made from local, seasonal produce. ££

Loudons

MAP PAGE 38

2 Sibbald Walk. www.loudons.co.uk.

Sleek, modern café plating up equally contemporary brunches. Think home-made muffin with avocado, chorizo and poached eggs topped with tomato and courgette salsa. ££

Mimi's Little Bakehouse

MAP PAGE 38

250 Canongate. www.mimisbake house.com.

Dinky, award-winning café specializing in cakes and scones – some of the lightest you'll ever taste. Generous breakfasts and lunches served, too. £

Tempo Tea Bar

MAP PAGE 38

7 East Market St. www.tempoteabar.com.

Friendly café specializing in bubble tea, a Taiwanese originated drink – made from green tea, milk, natural flavours and tapioca balls – that professes all manner of health benefits. £

Restaurants

Chop House Bar & Butchery

MAP PAGE 38

Arch 15, East Market St. www.chophouse steak.co.uk.

Residing in the beautifully converted arches beneath Jeffrey St, this sophisticated dining spot and watering hole is part tapas bar, part steakhouse. Cured meats and cheeses are regularly gifted at the bar, while more substantial lunches include the likes of steak and fries. £££

Vegetarian dining at David Bann

Monteiths restaurant and cocktail bar

David Bann Vegetarian Restaurant

MAP PAGE 38

56–58 St Mary's St. www.davidbann.co.uk.
A modern, plant-based twist on fine dining. Think gnocchi with pear salad or parsnip pudding with potato and swede dauphinoise. ££

La Garrigue

MAP PAGE 38

31 Jeffrey St. www.lagarrigue.co.uk.
A double AA Rosette-awarded restaurant, with a menu and wine list rooted in the produce and culinary traditions of the Languedoc region of France. For unmistakably authentic paysan cuisine, opt for the cassoulet. ££££

Ondine

MAP PAGE 38

2 George IV Bridge. www.ondine restaurant.co.uk.
Dedicated seafood restaurant from Edinburgh-born Roy Brett, once Rick Stein's main chef in Padstow, turning out sublime dishes using native shellfish and fish from sustainable sources. ££££

Wedgwood the Restaurant

MAP PAGE 38

267 Canongate. www.wedgwoodthe restaurant.co.uk.
This small, award-winning fine-dining restaurant with in-house forager draws on the natural larder of Scotland's land, rivers and seas and transforms it into inventive dishes worthy of a Michelin recommendation. Culinary genius comes with a high price tag, however, so opt for the excellent-value lunch menu if you have shallow pockets. ££££

The Witchery by the Castle

MAP PAGE 38

352 Castlehill. www.thewitchery.com.
An upmarket restaurant that only Edinburgh could create,

The Witchery by the Castle

set in magnificently over-the-top medieval surroundings full of Gothic wood panelling and heavy stonework, all a mere broomstick-hop from the Castle. The menu is as ostentatious as the surroundings, with wallet-draining lobster and lamb wellington on offer; however, there are good-value two-course set menus. ££££

Pubs and bars

The Banshee Labyrinth

MAP PAGE 38
29–35 Niddry St. www.thebanshee labyrinth.com.
"Scotland's most haunted pub" – apparently. While glasses have been known to shatter of their own accord, this impeccably dark and dingy bolthole is mostly haunted by metalheads and tourists. Built into a chunk of prime South Bridge vaults,

there are plenty of unsavoury nooks and crannies to enjoy the live metal, punk, occasional electronica, karaoke and B-movie cinema.

The City Café

MAP PAGE 38
19 Blair St. www.citycafeedinburgh.co.uk.
The American-diner-minimalist grand dame of Edinburgh style bars, and a home from home for fashionistas, wannabes and DJs in the late 80s and 90s. The competition may be much stiffer these days, but it's still a pre-club fixture.

Deacon Brodie's Tavern

MAP PAGE 38
435 Lawnmarket. www.nicholsons pubs.co.uk.
Lively, two-floored historic Victorian pub with a gorgeous ornate ceiling. Throngs with tourists and locals, particularly at lunchtime.

The Devil's Advocate
MAP PAGE 38

9 Advocates Close. www.devilsadvocate
edinburgh.co.uk.
Atmospheric bar in a converted
Victorian pumphouse hidden
halfway down a close and
specializing in exotic whisky. Tends
to fill at the end of the working day
with young office workers sipping
cocktails.

Halfway House
MAP PAGE 38

24 Fleshmarket Close. 0131 225 7101.
Formerly a second home for
Scotsman hacks when the
newspaper was based at South
Bridge, this tiny pub halfway up
the steep, narrow close between
the train station and the Royal
Mile, is a handy place to stop
and catch your breath. Lots of
real ales and a few simple bar
meals on offer, like sausage and
mash.

Jolly Judge
MAP PAGE 38

7 James Court. www.jollyjudge.co.uk.
Traditional pub tucked away in
a basement at the end of a windy
vennel that always has the big-
name Scottish ales on tap and,
come winter, an open fire in fine
fettle.

The Malt Shovel
MAP PAGE 38

11–15 Cockburn St. www.maltshovelinn-
edinburgh.co.uk.
Spacious Georgian-era pub on the
edge of the Old Town specializing
in whisky – there are over 150 on
offer. There's also a decent real ale
rotation and no-nonsense pub grub
available.

Salt Horse
MAP PAGE 38

57–61 Blackfriars St High St. www.salt
horse.beer.
A little off the beaten track, this
cosy bar with its own attached beer
shop specializes in craft brews from

around the world and also grills a
decent selection of burgers.

The Waverley
MAP PAGE 38

3–5 St Mary's St. www.waverleybar.co.uk.
Victorian charm oozes from
every crook and gnarl of
this one-time haunt of Billy
Connolly and Bert Jansch.
The folk music tradition is still
going strong here on Friday and
Saturday evenings as well as
Sunday mid-afternoons.

The World's End
MAP PAGE 38

2–8 High St. www.worldsend-edinburgh.
co.uk.
A rowdy old howf that gets its
name from the tolbooth that
used to sit outside, which was too
expensive for the poorest folk of
Edinburgh to pass through – hence
the name.

Clubs and venues

Monkey Barrel Comedy
MAP PAGE 38

9–11 Blair St. www.monkeybarrel
comedy.com.
Small, one-room venue
showcasing predominately new
and emerging acts. With entry
from £5 to £10 and a reasonably
priced bar, you're in for a cheap
night out.

Whistle Binkies
MAP PAGE 38

4–6 South Bridge. www.whistle
binkies.com.
An Edinburgh stalwart and one
of the most reliable places to
find live music every night of
the week (and often afternoons
too), or just to hunker down
in some of the lesser-haunted
South Bridge vaults. On the
whole, the venue hosts local
indie bands or rock and pop
covers, though there are some
folk evenings as well.

South of the Royal Mile

The southern section of the Old Town has two distinct levels. The upper belongs to a pair of Georgian bridges (George IV and South Bridge) that feed off from the Royal Mile; Chambers Street, home to the venerable National Museum of Scotland; and George Heriot's School, a glorious early seventeenth-century pile tucked inside the remnants of the old Flodden wall. To reach the lower section, most visitors find themselves enticed off the George IV Bridge by the curving incline of photogenic Victoria Street, with its colourful arched boutique shop fronts. At the foot of the hill, the street opens onto the Grassmarket, a large square filled with congenial pavement cafés, pubs and restaurants. In the early evenings, local barflies rub shoulders with hen and stag parties, who eventually stagger off to the late bars and clubs along the Cowgate to the east.

Victoria Street

MAP PAGE 56

Curving downhill from George IV Bridge towards the Grassmarket via West Bow, photogenic **Victoria Street** is an unusual two-tier thoroughfare, with colourful arcaded shops below and a

Colourful shops on Victoria Street

pedestrian terrace high above. The street has retained an aesthetic grip on itself, hosting a string of appealing offbeat, independent boutiques, a cheesemonger and an old bookseller.

Built between 1829 and 1834, Victoria Street was part of a series of improvements to the Old Town; access to Lawnmarket from the Grassmarket had previously been up a steep and often slippery incline at West Bow. All this changed with the mass demolition of rows of tenements all the way up today's Victoria Street to cut a path onto the newly built George IV Bridge.

The Grassmarket

MAP PAGE 56

Used as the city's cattle market from 1477 to 1911, the **Grassmarket** is an open, partly cobbled area, which despite being girdled by tall tenements offers an unexpected view north up to the precipitous walls of the Castle. Come springtime, it's often sunny enough for cafés to put tables and chairs along the pavement; however, such

Continental aspirations are a bit of a diversion as the Grassmarket is best remembered as the location of Edinburgh's public gallows – the spot is marked by a tiny garden. The notorious serial killers William Burke and William Hare had their lair in a now-vanished close just off the western end of the Grassmarket, and for a long time before its relatively recent gentrification there was a seamy edge to the place, filled with brothels and drinking dens.

The Grassmarket's two-sided character is still on view, with a lively drinking scene of an evening, while by day you can admire the architectural quirks and interesting shops and restaurants plus, on Saturdays, a food and craft market.

The Cowgate

MAP PAGE 56

Leading eastwards from the Grassmarket is the **Cowgate**, one of Edinburgh's oldest surviving streets. It was also once one of the city's most prestigious addresses, but the construction of the great **viaducts** of George IV Bridge and South Bridge entombed it below street level, condemning it to decay and neglect. Various nightclubs and Festival venues have established themselves here – on Friday and Saturday nights, the street heaves with revellers.

George Heriot's School

MAP PAGE 56

Laureston Place. www.george-heriots.com. Occasionally open to the public, check website for details. Free.

George Heriot's School was built with funds from the benevolent legacy of the namesake goldsmith-turned-philanthropist in the mid-seventeenth century to provide charitable education for poverty-stricken children. The resulting Renaissance building standing just west of the Greyfriars Kirk was the first large-scale construction outside of the city walls. Four main towers, each with four turrets, corner an inner quadrangle entered via the bell-topped clock tower on the north end. Its part castle, part palatial look became the inspiration for numerous other independent schools around the city and, more recently, Hogwarts

The Connolly Connection

Among Edinburgh's multitude of famous and infamous sons, one of the most obscure – and perhaps most unlikely – remains **James Connolly**, commander-in-chief of the **Easter 1916 rising** which eventually led to the formation of the Irish Republic. With no monument save for a small plaque at the foot of George IV Bridge in the Cowgate, few among Edinburgh's tourist hordes are likely aware that Connolly was born and raised there in the bowels of Edinburgh's Old Town. A pivotal figure in emerging socialist and trade union movements in Scotland, Ireland and beyond, including Keir Hardie's Independent Labour Party (a forerunner of the contemporary **Labour Party**), Connolly came to believe that armed insurrection was the only way to free Ireland from the British Empire, and his prominent role in the rising ultimately led to execution by firing squad (infamously while badly wounded and tied to a chair). While the uprising resulted in heavy casualties on both sides, as well as many civilian deaths, and the independent state that eventually emerged wasn't the socialist utopia he had dreamed of, his vision of freedom and equality for all has remained an inspiration to many.

from the *Harry Potter* series. Today, ironically, it's one of Edinburgh's more exclusive private schools and visiting is usually only possible during September's Open Doors day (www.doorsopendays.org.uk).

Anatomical Museum

MAP PAGE 56

Doorway 3, Medical School, Teviot Place. www.ed.ac.uk.

Edinburgh University's morbidly fascinating three-hundred-year-old collection is displayed at the **Anatomical Museum**. Expect phrenology masks, body sections and skeletal remains, including those of infamous serial killer William Burke, whose skin forms the cover of a notebook residing at the nearby Surgeons' Hall Museums (see page 59). Entered by passing between the two elephant skeletons standing in the splendid vaulted foyer, the museum is housed in a large, sky-lit rectangular room with numerous glass cabinets. There's a decent natural history contingent with a few primate skeletons and a huge narwhal's tooth, but the core of the collection relates to human anatomy. The gorier items, like its jarred foetal abnormalities, are locked away in the Skull Room (by prior arrangement if you can prove you are doing legitimate research).

Greyfriars Kirk

MAP PAGE 56

1 Greyfriars. www.greyfriarskirk.com. Free.

Greyfriars Kirk was built in 1620 on land that had belonged to a Franciscan convent, though little of the original late Gothic-style building remains. A fire in the mid-nineteenth century led to significant rebuilding and the installation of the first **organ** in a Presbyterian church in Scotland; today's magnificent instrument, by Peter Collins, arrived in 1990.

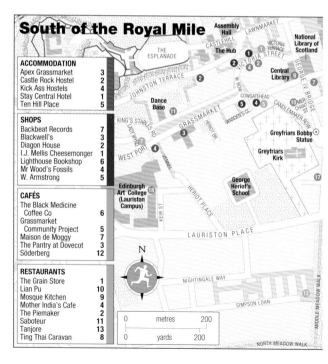

South of the Royal Mile

ACCOMMODATION

Apex Grassmarket	3
Castle Rock Hostel	2
Kick Ass Hostels	4
Stay Central Hotel	1
Ten Hill Place	5

SHOPS

Backbeat Records	7
Blackwell's	3
Diagon House	2
I.J. Mellis Cheesemonger	1
Lighthouse Bookshop	6
Mr Wood's Fossils	4
W. Armstrong	5

CAFÉS

The Black Medicine Coffee Co	6
Grassmarket Community Project	5
Maison de Moggy	7
The Pantry at Dovecot	3
Söderberg	12

RESTAURANTS

The Grain Store	1
Lian Pu	10
Mosque Kitchen	9
Mother India's Cafe	4
The Piemaker	2
Saboteur	11
Tanjore	13
Ting Thai Caravan	8

Greyfriars Bobby

The small statue of **Greyfriars Bobby,** at the junction of George IV Bridge and Candlemaker Row, must rank as one of Edinburgh's more mawkish tourist attractions. The legend goes that Bobby was a **Skye terrier** acquired as a working dog by a police constable named John Gray. When Gray died in 1858, Bobby was found a few days later sitting on his grave, a vigil he maintained until his death fourteen years later. In the process, he became an Edinburgh celebrity, fed and cared for by locals who gave him a special collar to prevent him being impounded as a stray. The statue was modelled from life and erected soon after his death. Bobby's legendary dedication easily lent itself to children's books and was eventually picked up by Disney, whose 1961 feature film hammed up the story and ensured that streams of tourists have paid their respects ever since.

Outside, the kirkyard has a fine collection of seventeenth-century gravestones and mausoleums, including the grave mourned over by the world-famous canine Greyfriars Bobby. Visited regularly by ghost tours, the kirkyard was known for **grave-robbing** as freshly interred bodies were exhumed and sold to the nearby medical school (a crime taken to a higher level by the notorious Burke and Hare, who bypassed the graveyards by simply murdering the victims before selling them). More

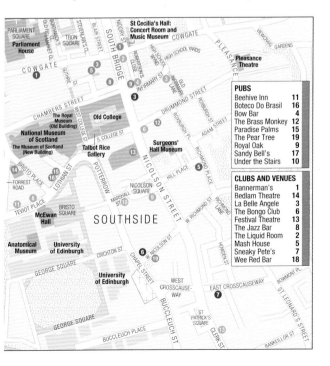

PUBS

Beehive Inn	11
Boteco Do Brasil	16
Bow Bar	4
The Brass Monkey	12
Paradise Palms	15
The Pear Tree	19
Royal Oak	9
Sandy Bell's	17
Under the Stairs	10

CLUBS AND VENUES

Bannerman's	1
Bedlam Theatre	14
La Belle Angele	3
The Bongo Club	6
Festival Theatre	13
The Jazz Bar	8
The Liquid Room	2
Mash House	5
Sneaky Pete's	7
Wee Red Bar	18

National Museum of Scotland

significantly, the kirkyard was the setting, in 1638, for the signing of the **National Covenant**, a dramatic act of defiance by the Presbyterian Scots against Charles I's attempts to impose episcopal worship on the country. In an undemocratic age, thousands of townsfolk and noblemen signed the original document at Greyfriars; copies were then made and sent around the country, with some 300,000 names being added.

National Museum of Scotland

MAP PAGE 56
Chambers St. www.nms.ac.uk. Free.
The **National Museum of Scotland** is essentially two distinct museums, internally connected to each other: the unorthodox **modern sandstone building** on the corner of George IV Bridge (the Museum of Scotland) houses collections of Scottish heritage, while the much older **Venetian-style palace** (the Royal Museum) offers a more global perspective of antiquity, geology and natural history. Inside, the wealth of exhibits is enough to occupy days of your time, but as entry is free,

you'll be able to dip in and out at leisure. Parents will also find the place a useful sanctuary since there are numerous child-friendly rooms, interactive exhibits and cafés.

The Royal Museum

MAP PAGE 56
Modelled on the former Crystal Palace in London, with a spectacular cast-iron interior, the **Old Building** packs in a bedazzling array of artefacts, covering natural history, world culture, geology and technology. The exhibits are housed over three levels surrounding the **Grand Gallery**, a huge central atrium whose beautiful limestone floor turns out to be teeming with fossils, predominantly ammonites. One standout exhibit, by the main concourse, is the gruesome **Millennium Clock Tower**, a jumble of cogs, chains and wheels modelled in the form of a Gothic cathedral, with gargoyles and sinister-looking figurines representing characters from twentieth-century politics.

The **Natural World Gallery** is particularly fine, too, inhabiting all tiers of the museum's eastern end with numerous recreated animals hanging top to bottom from the rafters and a fearsome T-rex skeleton at the entrance.

The Museum of Scotland

MAP PAGE 56

Given its confusing and unconventional layout, the **Scottish galleries** are best explored with a map (free from the entrance) in hand. The newer **Museum of Scotland** details the history of the country, from its geological formation through to the present day. In between, there's a wealth of remarkably well-preserved medieval exhibits – religious, regal and day-to-day objects – on display in the **Kingdom of the Scots**, including the exquisitely idiosyncratic **Lewis chessmen**. Moving forward in time, **Scotland Transformed** offers an insight into the Union of Crowns and the crushed Jacobite rebellions, leading up to the Industrial Revolution – evoked by an unmissable life-size working model of a steam-driven Newcomen Atmospheric Engine. Designed in 1712, it foreshadows Scotland's role as covered in the next section, **Industry and Empire**, where you can see a full-size steam locomotive, the *Ellesmere*, highlighting the fact that nineteenth-century Scotland was building more railway engines than anywhere else in the world.

Surgeons' Hall Museum

MAP PAGE 56

Nicolson St, between nos. 14 & 16. www.museum.rcsed.ac.uk. Charge.
Surgeons' Hall, the former headquarters of the Royal College of Surgeons, is a handsome, iconic temple with a stately columned facade built by William Playfair (1790–1857), one of Edinburgh's greatest architects. Housed round the back is one of the city's most unusual and morbidly compelling museums. In the eighteenth and nineteenth centuries, Edinburgh was a leading centre of medical

and anatomical research, nurturing world-famous pioneers such as James Young Simpson, founder of anaesthesia, and Joseph Lister, the father of modern surgery. The **history of surgery** takes up one part of the museum, with intriguing exhibits ranging from early surgical tools to a pocketbook covered with the leathered skin of serial killer William Burke. Another room has a curation of gruesome instruments illustrating the history of dentistry, while the third and most remarkable part of the museum, the elegant **Playfair Hall**, contains an array of specimens and jars from the college's eighteenth-century anatomical and pathological collections.

Old College and Talbot Rice Gallery

MAP PAGE 56

South Bridge. www.trg.ed.ac.uk. Free.
Designed by Edinburgh's famous New Town architects, Robert Adam and, after he died, William Playfair, the resulting **Old College** is an aesthetically pleasing symmetrical orgy of sandstone, pillars, arcades and domes surrounding a featureless quadrangle.

At the far end of the building is the University's **Talbot Rice Gallery**, set up in the seventies to foster links and collaborations between students, academics and world-renowned artists. For the visitor there are three distinct exhibition spaces of predominately contemporary art on show. Gallery one concentrates on new solo exhibitions on a certain theme, usually by a Scottish artist. Gallery two, with its glass cupola and rich Georgian interior, is the most eye-catching, and the displays here are historic, academic and experimental. Highlights include the university's Torrie Collection, a body of nineteenth-century work ranging from Dutch and Flemish landscapes to Renaissance bronzes. Gallery three is dedicated to supporting emerging and experimental artists.

Shops

Backbeat Records

MAP PAGE 56

31 East Crosscauseway. 0131 668 2666.

Small vinyl-enthusiast's shop jam-packed with approaching 100,000 records and almost no room to manoeuvre.

Blackwell's

MAP PAGE 56

53–62 South Bridge. www.blackwell.co.uk.

Rambling, multifloored bookseller with a strong – though far from exclusive – focus on academic tomes. You'll also find many volumes and travel guides relating to Scotland.

Diagon House

MAP PAGE 56

40 Victoria St. 0131 226 5882.

An essential stop for any Harry Potter devotee looking for wands, capes, stuffed owls or scarves. Keep an eye out for the large Nagini snake dangling from the ceiling.

I.J. Mellis Cheesemonger

MAP PAGE 56

30a Victoria St, Old Town.

www.mellischeese.net.

Founded in 1993, Mellis' Old Town shop is charmingly kitted out in a Victorian style and well stocked with expertly conditioned farmhouse and artisan cheeses from Britain, Ireland and, to a lesser extent, the Continent as well as a small selection of jamón, chorizo and bread.

Lighthouse Bookshop

MAP PAGE 56

43–45 W Nicolson St. www.lighthouse bookshop.com.

Queer-owned and women-led indie bookshop championing marginalized voices and celebrating diversity. A great spot to pick up feminist, antiracist and LGBTQ+ titles; ask the team for recommendations, they really know their stuff.

Mr Wood's Fossils

MAP PAGE 56

5 Cowgatehead. www.mrwoodsfossils. co.uk.

An internationally acclaimed dealer in fossils, ambers, meteorites and jewellery. The displays are fascinating and extensive, with items to suit all budgets from cheap ammonites to budget-blowing dinosaur bones.

W. Armstrong

MAP PAGE 56

83 Grassmarket. www.armstrongsvintage. co.uk.

A treasure trove of vintage and retro fashion, this small chain is like a museum; stuffed to the gunwales with items encompassing everything from pre-war civvies to the static-inducing nylon wear of the 1970s.

Cafés

The Black Medicine Coffee Co

MAP PAGE 56

2 Nicholson St. www.blackmed.co.uk.

Just adjacent to Edinburgh Uni's Old College, this cosy coffee shop with its attractive Victorian interior and handcrafted wooden tables is a hub for the resident academics. £

Grassmarket Community Project

MAP PAGE 56

86 Candlemaker Row.

www.grassmarket.org.

Appealing not-for-profit café in the purpose-built local community centre providing excellent home-made cakes and light lunches. The interior is all white and bright thanks to the double-storey glass frontage and roof lights. £

Maison de Moggy

MAP PAGE 56

17–19 West Port. www.maisondemoggy.com. Charge for entry, under-10s not allowed. Reservation advised.

Edinburgh's contribution to the cat-café craze, this niche redoubt allows you to pass one therapeutic hour – the length of each session – with a clowder of pedigree pussycats and a cup of locally produced coffee. £

The Pantry at Dovecot

MAP PAGE 56

10 Infirmary St. www.dovecotstudios.com.

Contemporary artisan café with attached and affiliated art gallery. Serves healthy light lunches of soups, salads and sandwiches plus excellent coffee. £

Söderberg

MAP PAGE 56

27 Simpson Loan. www.soderberg.uk.

A Swedish outfit with bread ovens on view, baskets of loaves and buns out front and the best coffee in town. £

Restaurants

The Grain Store

MAP PAGE 56

30 Victoria St. www.grainstore-restaurant.co.uk.

Decades-long Victoria Street fixture and a haven amid the bustle of the Old Town, with intimate stone walls and soft lighting. Combines top-quality modern Scottish and French cuisines; lunches (good-value three-course set menu available) include the likes of hake and red mullet in a fennel and ginger broth. ££££

Lian Pu

MAP PAGE 56

14 Marshall St. 0131 662 8895.

Thoroughly hip fast-food haunt popular among Edinburgh's Chinese student community, thanks to its true home-from-home cooking and palatable prices. Try the seafood cooked in a clay pot or dunk a red bean paste stuffed steamed bun into a steaming bowl of tomato and egg soup. £

The Grain Store restaurant

Mosque Kitchen

MAP PAGE 56

Edinburgh Central Mosque, 50 Potterrow
(entrance on West Nicholson St). 0131
629 1630.

Out of the many "curry in a hurry"
establishments that are cropping up
around the Nicholson Street area,
this is a true time-served veteran.
Tagged onto the mosque, this no-
nonsense canteen has for years been
dishing out glorious, hugely filling
plates of rice and curry for under a
tenner. £

Mother India's Cafe

MAP PAGE 56

3–5 Infirmary St. www.motherindia.co.uk.

Tapas with a twist – so the
restaurant slogan goes. The twist:
the tapas is Indian, not Spanish. A
novel concept, though the menu
won't trouble seasoned curry
connoisseurs, with classics like daal
makhani and chicken tikka on
offer. ££

The Piemaker

MAP PAGE 56

38 South Bridge. www.thepiemaker.co.uk.

Possibly the cheapest place to fill up
in town, with a mightily impressive
range of pies, from carnivore to
vegan plus a few sweet ones. £

Saboteur

MAP PAGE 56

19–20 Teviot Place. www.saboteur
restaurant.com.

Vietnamese street food popular
with a young crowd, who perch
on wooden stools and slurp
down bowls of pho and shares
plates of bao buns, roti and
dumplings. Sister restaurant to
Ting Thai Caravan, on the same
street, so if you can't get a seat
in one – try the other. ££

Tanjore

MAP PAGE 56

6–8 Clerk St. www.tanjore.co.uk.

The finest ambassador for South
Indian cuisine on these shores,
drawing in all the regional

standards including *vadai*
(crunchy lentil doughnuts), *idli*
(rice and lentil cake) and *sambar*
– a distinctly rich, savoury
curry with fragrant, bittersweet
curry leaves. The freshly made
dosai (lentil and rice crêpes) are
among the lightest and crispiest
you'll ever taste and come with a
wide variety of fillings. ££

Ting Thai Caravan

MAP PAGE 56

10 Hill Place. www.tingthaicaravan.com.

Edinburgh's number-one street-
food destination with queues
regularly out the door, partly
due to the no-reservation policy
but also the restaurant's culinary
authenticity and its cosy, social
ambiance. Another draw might be
the rock-bottom prices. Crowd-
pleasers include the Bangkok
spicy chicken wings and the crispy
fried noodles with seafood in a
massaman broth. £

Pubs

Beehive Inn

MAP PAGE 56

18–20 Grassmarket. www.belhavenpubs.
co.uk.

One of the few family-friendly
pubs in the centre. Inside, it's a
beautiful early Victorian former
coaching inn with high-backed
red leather seating and corniced
ceilings in each of its three rooms.

Boteco Do Brasil

MAP PAGE 56

47 Lothian St. www.botecodobrasil.com.

Popular Brazilian themed bar with
a menu of colourful cocktails and
street-food tapas. Look out for live
samba music sessions or the salsa
and bachata dance lessons.

Bow Bar

MAP PAGE 56

80 West Bow. www.thebowbar.co.uk.

Wonderful old wood-panelled
bar and one of the nicest, most

convivial drinking spots in the city centre, though it does get uncomfortably busy at weekends. Staff really know their whiskies, so ask for advice if you're struggling to decide which of the 150-strong collection to order. Also a changing selection of first-rate Scottish and English cask beers, plus decent pies too.

The Brass Monkey

MAP PAGE 56
14 Drummond St. www.brassmonkey edinburgh.co.uk.
Popular boozer with students thanks to its cheap drinks, regular pub quizzes and daily 3pm film screenings (free) in the cosy back room.

Paradise Palms

MAP PAGE 56
41 Lothian St. www.theparadisepalms.com.
In a location that has seen countless bars come and go over the decades, *Paradise Palms* has firmly established itself as perhaps the capital's most painfully hip outpost. A tropical-thriftstore-cum-cabaret-lounge theme; vegan and veggie

takes on Deep South soul food (like the finger lickin' southern fried seitan); and even a vinyl store and electronica-oriented record label are all part of the appeal.

The Pear Tree

MAP PAGE 56
38 West Nicolson St. www.peartree edinburgh.co.uk.
Though this Edinburgh landmark recently had its character all but obliterated in a needless makeover, the eighteenth-century exterior – with two beautiful old pear trees trained on its west wall – is still a sight for sore eyes. Its greatest asset has always been its large, cobbled courtyard – one of central Edinburgh's very few bona-fide beer gardens, routinely rammed come summer, with live bands and barbecues.

Royal Oak

MAP PAGE 56
1 Infirmary St. www.royal-oak-folk.com.
Traditional Scottish pub hosting daily informal folk sessions performed by locals. On Sundays, there's the "Wee Folk Club" (charge

The Bow Bar

for entry) from 8.30pm, hosting soloists or groups from around the country and beyond.

Sandy Bell's

MAP PAGE 56

25 Forrest Rd. www.sandybellsedinburgh. co.uk. Entry free.

A truly legendary, richly atmospheric and strictly traditional folk music bar that's been doing its thing since the 1940s. Famous for fine ales, malt whiskies and a good old singsong, it's one of the last of its kind in the capital.

Under the Stairs

MAP PAGE 56

3a Merchant St. www.underthestairs.org.

Comfy, shabby-chic bar with great cocktails, popular with the pre-clubbing crowd. Food served late, with sharing plates of cheese or charcuterie available right up until closing time.

Clubs and venues

Bannerman's

MAP PAGE 56

212 Cowgate. www.bannermanslive.co.uk.

Charge for entry.

Another stalwart on Edinburgh's live music scene, with a labyrinth of caves and musky warrens located at the base of South Bridge. The most atmospheric joint in town to catch local indie bands hoping for a big break.

Bedlam Theatre

MAP PAGE 56

11 Bristol Place. www.bedlamtheatre. co.uk.

The oldest entirely student-run theatre in Britain, this deconsecrated neo-Gothic church hosts over forty different performances annually.

La Belle Angele

MAP PAGE 56

11 Hasties Close, Cowgate. www.la-belle angele.com.

A legendary 90s venue that recently rose from the ashes, quite literally, after it was burned to the ground in a 2002 fire. The venue hosted Radiohead, Oasis and some of the city's best club nights back in the day. In its new incarnation, the likes of Craig Charles and Leftfield have shown up for DJ

Festival Theatre

sets, while the venue's rota flips between tribute bands, retro nights, reggaeton and jungle.

The Bongo Club

MAP PAGE 56

66 Cowgate. www.thebongoclub.co.uk. Charge for entry.

An iconic, peripatetic Edinburgh club and arts venue with an eclectic and experimental line-up. Look out for the monthly grime and dubstep night Electrikal; funk and Latin fixture Soulsville!; and immortal reggae institution Messenger Sound System, which has outlasted (by decades) almost every other club night in the city.

Festival Theatre

MAP PAGE 56

13–29 Nicolson St. www.capital theatres.com.

The largest stage in Britain, principally used for the Scottish Opera and Scottish Ballet's appearances in the capital, but also for everything from cinematic festivals to circus performances.

The Jazz Bar

MAP PAGE 56

1a Chambers St. www.thejazzbar.co.uk. Charge after 7pm.

There's been a subterranean jazz bar on this site for decades, more or less. The current incarnation (set up by the late jazz drummer Bill Kyle in 2005) hosts up to five performances a day, every day, with an eclectic roster and a generous definition of jazz seeing soul, funk, blues and electronica all getting a look-in. All door money goes directly to the musicians.

The Liquid Room

MAP PAGE 56

9c Victoria St. www.liquidroom.com. Charge for club night (sometimes free before 11pm).

Another club and live-music venue with a long and chequered history that has, in its time, played host to luminaries as diverse as Mogwai,

John Martyn, Kelis, The Beta Band, Grandmaster Flash, Nancy Sinatra and Franz Ferdinand. These days, it's home to indie superclub franchise Propaganda, a fair dose of tribute bands, cutting-edge touring acts such as Black Midi as well as the occasional rock legend like Creedence Clearwater Revival.

Mash House

MAP PAGE 56

37 Guthrie St (entrance up Hastie's Close from the Cowgate). www.themashhouse. co.uk. Charge for entry.

Sequestered away in a side-street hidey-hole just off the Cowgate, this is regarded as one of the best venues in the city among bands, promoters, DJs and punters, and has hosted the likes of Andrew Weatherall. The downstairs dancefloor is just the right size for working up a sweat, especially when Samedia are in town (usually first Sat of month) with their trademark blend of tropical bass.

Sneaky Pete's

MAP PAGE 56

73 Cowgate. www.sneakypetes.co.uk. Charge for entry.

Condensed sweat and a fiercely eclectic roster characterize this 100-capacity Cowgate perennial, often cited as the soul of the capital's grassroots scene. Club nights such as Coalition and Teesh are solid fixtures, while the tiny stage has hosted everyone from seminal DJ Bill Brewster to veteran Japanese psyche-rockers Acid Mothers Temple.

Wee Red Bar

MAP PAGE 56

Edinburgh Art College, Lauriston Place. www.weeredbar.co.uk. Charge for entry.

This art college legend may be small but its history is long: monthly club night The Egg is to indie music what the Bongo's Messenger (see page 64) is to reggae.

Holyrood and Arthur's Seat

At the foot of Canongate lies Holyrood, for centuries known as Edinburgh's royal quarter, with its ruined thirteenth-century abbey and the Palace of Holyroodhouse. Over the past few decades, however, the area has been transformed by the addition of Enric Miralles' highly controversial Scottish Parliament, a love-it or loathe-it concrete monolith "almost surging out of the rock" – as Miralles put it – of adjacent Arthur's Seat. This extinct volcano remains the centrepiece of Holyrood Park, a natural wilderness in the heart of the modern city comprising a stunning variety of landscapes. You can sit in the lee of Arthur's Seat, in the centre of the glen, and not see a single high-rise nor indeed any trace of urban life – incredible for a major European capital.

Holyrood Distillery

MAP PAGE 68
19 St Leonard's Ln. www.holyrood
distillery.co.uk. Charge for tours.

The first (for nearly 100 years) in the wave of independent, artisanal breweries springing up across Edinburgh, housed in an early Victorian former railway goods shed. Opened in 2019, the single malt whisky distillery offers an array of excellent tours and experiences, including a paired tasting of whiskies and beers from Edinburgh's craft breweries. Also has a gin distillery, a bar with huge windows framing views of Holyrood Park, and a spirits and gift shop. In June, it hosts The Mash Up, an annual festival celebrating whisky, gin, beer and food.

The Palace of Holyroodhouse

MAP PAGE 68
Canongate. www.rct.uk. Charge; joint
tickets available with Queen's Gallery.

In its present form, the **Palace of Holyroodhouse** is largely a seventeenth-century creation, planned for Charles II. However, the tower house of the old palace (the sole survivor of a fire during Oliver Cromwell's occupation) built for James V in 1532 was skilfully incorporated to form the northwestern block of today's building, with a virtual mirror image of it erected as a counterbalance at the other end.

Tours of the palace move through a series of royal **reception rooms** featuring some outstanding encrusted plasterwork, each more impressive than the last, an idea Charles II had picked up from his cousin Louis XIV's Versailles. On the northern side of the internal quadrangle, the **Great Gallery** extends almost the full length of the palace and is dominated by portraits of 96 Scottish kings, painted by Jacob de Wet in 1684 to illustrate the lineage of Stewart royalty.

As you move into the oldest part of the palace, known as **James V's tower**, the formal, ceremonial tone gives way to dark medieval history, with a tight spiral staircase leading to the chambers used by **Mary, Queen of Scots**. These contain various relics, though the most compelling viewing is a tiny supper room, from where in 1566 Mary's Italian secretary, **David Rizzio**, was dragged by conspirators, including her jealous husband, Lord Darnley, to the outer chamber and stabbed 56 times.

Holyrood Abbey

MAP PAGE 68
www.historicenvironment.scot/visit-a-place/places/holyrood-abbey. Free tour included in palace ticket on a "turn-up-and-go" basis; joint tickets available with Palace of Holyroodhouse and Queen's Gallery ticket, which also includes history tour of formal palace gardens.

Standing beside the palace are the evocative ruins of **Holyrood Abbey**, some of which date back to the thirteenth century. Gutted in 1688 by an anti-Catholic mob, the roof finally tumbled down in 1768. The melancholy scene inspired Felix Mendelssohn, who in 1829 wrote: "Everything is in ruins and mouldering … I believe I have found the beginning of my Scottish Symphony there today." Adjacent to the abbey are the formal palace gardens, open to visitors during the summer months. Plans are afoot to recreate both the palace's pioneering, seventeenth-century **physic garden** (the original cue for

Edinburgh's Royal Botanic Garden) and a flowering meadow inspired by the abbey's fifteenth-century monastic garden.

Queen's Gallery

MAP PAGE 68
Canongate. www.rct.uk. Charge; joint tickets available with Palace of Holyroodhouse.

Essentially an adjunct to the Palace of Holyroodhouse, the **Queen's Gallery** is located in a former church directly between the palace and the Scottish Parliament. With just two principal viewing rooms, it's a compact space, but has an appealing contemporary style. The gallery is temporarily closed until 2024 for maintenance work. Usually, it displays changing exhibitions from the **Royal Collection**, a vast array of art treasures held by the Royal Family on behalf of the British nation. Recent displays have included a remarkable collection of Leonardo da Vinci's drawings and scribblings showing the extent of the great masters' interests ranging from engineering and cartography to botany and anatomy.

The ruins of Holyrood Abbey

Garden Lobby, Scottish Parliament

The Scottish Parliament

MAP PAGE 68
Horse Wynd. www.visitparliament.scot.
Free guided tours (1hr); booking is
recommended (access is limited to lobby
and debating chamber if unguided); also
free creche.

The most controversial public
building to be erected in Scotland
since World War II, the **Scottish
Parliament** houses the country's
directly elected assembly, which
reconvened in 1999 for the first
time in almost 300 years (see page
153). Anvil-shaped panels clad
the exterior and the extraordinary
windows of the offices are shaped
like the profile of a mountain or a
section of the Forth Rail Bridge.
While the stark concrete interior
makes it look unfinished, there are
moments where grace and boldness
collide, exemplified by the **Garden
Lobby**, with a fascinating roof of
glass panels forming the shape of
an upturned boat.

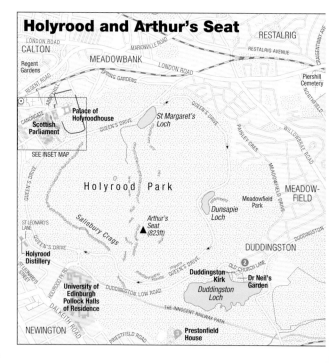

There's free access into the building's **entrance lobby**, where you'll find a small exhibition providing some historical, political and architectural background. If Parliament is in session, it's normally possible to watch proceedings in the **debating chamber** from the public gallery, though you have to get a pass from the front desk in the lobby. To see the rest of the interior properly, you'll need to join one of the highly recommended **regular guided tours**. Special tours dedicated to the architecture of the building and its collection of contemporary Scottish art also take place, albeit much less frequently – check the website for details.

Dynamic Earth

MAP PAGE 68
112 Holyrood Rd. www.dynamicearth.co.uk. Charge.

Beneath a pincushion of white metal struts that make it look like a miniature version of London's Millennium Dome, **Dynamic Earth** is a hi-tech, immersive attraction based on the wonders of the natural world and aimed at families with kids between 5 and 15. **Galleries** cover the formation of the earth and continents with crashing sound effects and a shaking floor, while the calmer grandeur of glaciers and oceans is explored through magnificent large-screen landscape footage. Further on, the polar regions – complete with a real iceberg – and tropical jungles are imaginatively recreated, with interactive computer screens and special effects at every turn.

Relief for scienced-out parents is at hand via the occasional **Dome Nights** event (check website for upcoming shows), hosting the likes of Pink Floyd's

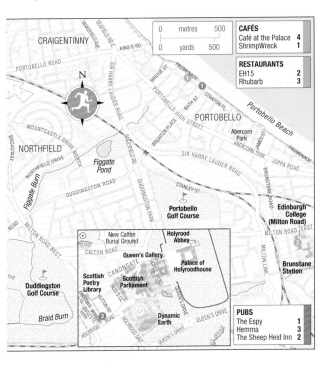

CAFÉS	
Café at the Palace	4
ShrimpWreck	1

RESTAURANTS	
EH15	2
Rhubarb	3

PUBS	
The Espy	1
Hemma	3
The Sheep Heid Inn	2

Dark Side of the Moon beamed around the dome in its entirety, complete with obligatory cosmic visuals.

Holyrood Park

MAP PAGE 68

Packing a dazzling array of landscapes – hills, crags, moorland, marshes, glens, lochs and fields – into 650 acres, **Holyrood Park** is Scotland in miniature. Once a royal hunting estate, it was given park status in the sixteenth century by King James V. While old photographs of the park show crops growing and sheep grazing, it's now used mostly by outdoor enthusiasts. A single tarred road, **Queen's Drive**, loops through the park, perfect for a circular cycle route.

Salisbury Crags

MAP PAGE 68

The sheer cliff face of **Salisbury Crags** is one of Edinburgh's most formidable natural features, climbing high above the Canongate and offering up an unforgettable view of Edinburgh, the Pentland Hills and fringes of Fife, especially at sunset. An easy hour-long circular route begins across from Holyroodhouse; a path called "The Radical Road" (see page 70) winds southwards across the crags for a little under a mile before you have the opportunity to hike north through the glen separating them

from Arthur's Seat and back to your starting point.

Arthur's Seat

MAP PAGE 68

The usual starting point for the ascent of **Arthur's Seat** which, at 823ft above sea level, towers above Edinburgh's numerous high points, is just across from the car park at Holyrood Palace, or – if you're driving – from Dunsapie Loch. Part of a volcano that last saw action 350 million years ago, its connections to the legendary king are fairly sketchy: the name is likely to be a corruption of the Gaelic *Ard-na-said*, or "height of arrows". From the Palace, it's a 30–40min walk/climb up grassy slopes to the rocky summit. On a clear day, views might just stretch to the English border and the Atlantic Ocean. While the summit can get very crowded, there are any number of quiet trails snaking all over the lower hills – don't be afraid to get off the beaten path and explore.

Duddingston Village

MAP PAGE 68

The beguiling conservation village of **Duddingston**, below the southeastern flanks of Arthur's Seat some 2.5 miles from the city centre, is attractively strung along the shores of **Duddingston Loch** – best known as the setting for Henry Raeburn's *Reverend Robert Walker Skating on Duddingston Loch*, on show at the National Gallery (see

The Radical Road

In a city of conspicuously royalist street names, **The Radical Road**, high up on Salisbury Crags (see page 70), stands defiantly apart, the name deriving from the **Radical War** of 1820, in which Glaswegian weavers rose up against social injustice and exploitation. Inevitably, the rebellion was mercilessly crushed, and its leaders hung. Ever eager to do his bit for king and country, **Walter Scott** subsequently suggested that the jobless weavers be put to work paving a path through the Crags, their political sympathies ultimately christening their toil.

Duddingston Loch

page 79). Most visitors come here for a stiff drink at the historic *Sheep Heid Inn* (see page 73) after hiking down from Arthur's Seat, and there's no more appealing place to escape the city's bustle. A plaque on the handsome (private) house at no.8–10 The Causeway, records it as the site of **Bonnie Prince Charlie's Council of War** prior to his routing of government troops at the Battle of Prestonpans in September 1745.

Dr Neil's Garden

MAP PAGE 68

Old Church Lane. www.drneilsgarden.co.uk. Free (donation welcome). Bus #42.

Completely secluded behind the twelfth-century Duddingston Kirk and accessed via a gate in the high stone walls of Old Church Lane is **Dr Neil's Garden**, one of Edinburgh's – and perhaps one of Scotland's – best-kept secrets. This truly special place comprises a lattice of cobbled paths, stone benches and contemplative nooks and crannies, bordered by hardy shrubs and alpine flowers, and shaded by musky Scots pine punctuated with rarities like North America sequoia and Chilean araucaria (monkey puzzle), all sloping down to ravishing views of Duddingston Loch and its rich birdlife. Created out of rocky grazing land over just a few decades by a husband-and-wife team of GPs, the garden fulfilled a dual function of recreation and healing, with their patients encouraged to tend it and partake of the tranquil air. Even today, it places an emphasis on wellbeing and welcomes volunteers.

Portobello

MAP PAGE 68

Among Edinburgh's least-expected assets is its **beach**, a mile-long stretch of golden sand, most of which falls within **Portobello**, or "Porty" in local parlance, a suburb around three miles east of the centre of town (bus #15 or #26 eastbound from Princes St). As well as a fiercely independent and community-minded spirit, it retains a certain wind-bleached charm thanks to a cluster of attractive Victorian buildings and its delightful promenade. On hot summer weekends, the beach can be a mass of swimmers, sunbathers, surfers and pleasure boats.

Cafés

Café at the Palace

MAP PAGE 68

Canongate. www.rct.uk.

The rarefied setting of the glass-roofed Palace Mews and Courtyard at Holyroodhouse makes for a suitably genteel backdrop to a classic afternoon tea, served in specially commissioned china; if you're feeling particularly regal, treat yourself to the champagne option. ££££

ShrimpWreck

MAP PAGE 68

Portobello. www.shrimpwreck.co.uk.

From an itinerant pop-up street-food truck, *ShrimpWreck* opened its first permanent base on Portobello's waterfront in 2021 – and hasn't looked back since. Daily specials and firm favourites are scribbled in chalk on a blackboard outside the wooden seafood shack: crab mac and cheese, shrimp buns, lobster rolls, seafood chowder – best

Café at the Palace

enjoyed on the beach overlooking the Firth of Forth. £

Restaurants

EH15

MAP PAGE 68

The Club, 24 Milton Road East, Portobello. www.edinburghcollege.ac.uk/restaurants/EH15.

Gourmet grub on a budget as college catering students test their culinary mettle – the three-course set lunch menu is a real bargain at £12, while the set menu in the evening is a wallet-friendly £25. Inevitably hit-and-miss but chances are you'll eat like a food critic for the price of a takeaway, and the wraparound, fifth-floor views are sensational. ££

Rhubarb

MAP PAGE 68

Prestonfield House, Priestfield Rd. www.prestonfield.com/dine/rhubarb.

Ensconced in glorious pastoral isolation among the red-and-

Café at the Palace

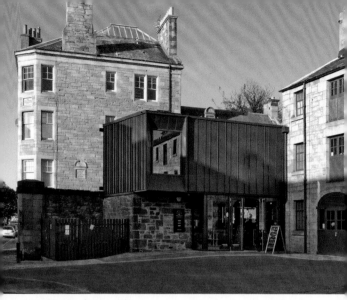

Holyrood Distillery (see page 66)

gold floral riot of A-listed *Prestonfield House* hotel, this place is tailor-made for a lavish romantic dinner. Locally sourced and gourmet the food may be, but it's not above a humble plate of rhubarb crumble and custard either – Prestonfield Estate being the first in Scotland to grow the tart-flavoured vegetable. ££££

Pubs

The Espy

MAP PAGE 68
62–64 Bath Street, Portobello. www.bit.ly/the-espy.
Hugely popular Porty bar, crammed with kitsch and beloved of locals (and their dogs), beachcombers and families, and serving up a full menu of fairly typical bar food, as well as cocktails and milkshakes.

Hemma

MAP PAGE 68
Tunbuilding, 73 Holyrood Road. www.bodabar.com/hemma.

Plate-glass brutalism meets Scandi chic at family-friendly *Hemma*. Sip a cocktail in one of the mismatched chairs and order a plate of Swedish meatballs, creamy mash and lingonberry jam to soak up the booze.

The Sheep Heid Inn

MAP PAGE 68
43–45 The Causeway, Duddingston. www.thesheepheidedinburgh.co.uk.
No less than Scotland's oldest – and possibly most famous – pub and one-time watering hole to, variously, Mary, Queen of Scots, King James VI and Bonnie Prince Charlie, the *Sheep Heid* is said to have first opened its doors in 1360. This impeccable historical pedigree is complemented by a charming courtyard beer garden, a nineteenth-century skittle alley and a menu of reasonable gastro-grub. Queen Elizabeth II left locals gobsmacked when she turned up out of the blue for a meal in 2016, eating out in public being something she rarely did, even in London.

Princes Street

Running parallel to and north of the historic Royal Mile, Edinburgh's main shopping artery, Princes Street, must surely rank as one of the most picturesque in the world. Its mile-long stretch of High Street chain stores clustered only along the north side of the street gaze out to the jagged silhouette of the Old Town and Castle, while to the east views take in the 200ft Scott Monument, the late Victorian *Balmoral Hotel* and beyond to the extinct volcanoes of Calton Hill and Arthur's Seat. Originally a residential street named in honour of King George IV's sons, few of Princes Street's original buildings survive; most were displaced by the medley of retail outlets that sprung up during the Victorian era and beyond. Luckily, the delightful residents' gardens across the street were retained and opened to the public.

General Register House

MAP PAGE 76
2 Princes St. www.nrscotland.gov.uk. Free with a Reader's ticket.

Designed in 1774 by Robert Adam, the **General Register House** is the most distinguished building on Princes Street. Today, it's home to the **Scotland's People Centre**, a dedicated family history unit that acts as a single point of access for those researching genealogical records. To visit, you will need to bring two forms of ID and two passport-sized photographs in order to obtain a free Reader's

General Register House on Princes Street

ticket. Once that's out of the way, you can pore over a mixed archive of records ranging from national censuses to criminal records and, stretching back to 1553, old parish registers of births, marriages and deaths. A large database complements the physical records and there are computers for public use if you don't have your own. Part of the appeal of embarking on some research is the opportunity to spend time in the elegant interior, centred on a glorious rotunda, lavishly decorated with plasterwork and antique-style medallions.

St James Quarter

MAP PAGE 76
St James Square. www.stjames
quarter.com.

The much-anticipated **St James Quarter** finally opened a sizeable chunk of the new 850,000-square-ft shopping galleria in 2021, after five years in the making. A gaggle of high-street stores caters to shoppers, who are kept fed by local food pop-ups on Little King Street. For eats with a view, *Duck & Waffle* (see page 82) looms over the city, with an outdoor terrace for cocktails, while the *W Edinburgh* (see page 140) will bring the esteemed hotel brand to Scotland for the first time when it opens in late 2023. The enclave is set to become a cultural centre, with a string of events spaces and impending partnerships with the likes of Fringe Festival. Elsewhere, there is the *Bonnie & Wild* food hall (www.bonnieandwildmarket. com), home to the excellent *Creel Caught* and its famed Arbroath smokies; a boutique Everyman cinema; and *Roomzzz Aparthotel* (see page 140).

Edinburgh Street Food

MAP PAGE 76
OMNi Centre, Leith St. www.edinburgh-
street-food.com.

Foodies rejoice, the city now has its first permanent daily street-food

Balmoral Hotel

market. Taking over a 900-square-metre corner of the OMNi Centre, **Edinburgh Street Food** opened in 2023 close to the new St James Quarter. The epicurean enclave is home to ten food vendors, including locals' favourite *Junk*, whose inventive chefs reimagine fine dining with a cool twist; award-winning East Asian fusion haunt *Bundits*, famed for its fluffy Hirata bao; and *Antojitos*, which turns out delicious plant-based Mexican food. There's a covered outdoor dining space for up to 250 guests.

Balmoral Hotel

MAP PAGE 76
1 Princes St. www.roccofortehotels.com.
A time capsule of late Victorian splendour, the massive baronial-style building and clock tower standing proud at Princes Street's east end is one of Edinburgh's most iconic landmarks. The city's most luxurious hotel, the **Balmoral** – meaning 'majestic dwelling' in Gaelic – boasts a fine-dining restaurant, a pool, spa and suites that can set you back as much as £4000 a night. The final Harry Potter book, *The Deathly Hallows*

St James Quarter

was famously penned in room 552, since renamed, the 'J.K. Rowling Suite'. Outside, the clock tower faithfully tells the wrong time; it's been set three minutes fast since 1902 to help passengers catch their trains on time at the station below.

The Edinburgh Dungeon

MAP PAGE 76
31 Market St. www.thedungeons.com/edinburgh. Charge.

Edinburgh's tourist industry gets decent mileage from the villains and ghosts of the city's medieval past but none more so than the **Edinburgh Dungeon**. This family-friendly attraction puts on a theatrical guided tour of subterranean chambers that include a torture room, an anatomy theatre and plenty of stories of old Edinburgh with accompanying special effects as well as couple of joyfully macabre rides.

The Fruitmarket Gallery

MAP PAGE 76
45 Market St. www.fruitmarket.co.uk. Free.

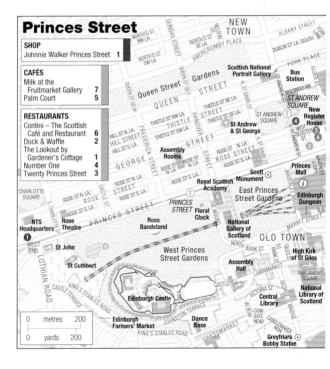

Princes Street

SHOP
Johnnie Walker Princes Street 1

CAFÉS
Milk at the Fruitmarket Gallery 7
Palm Court 5

RESTAURANTS
Contini – The Scottish Café and Restaurant 6
Duck & Waffle 2
The Lookout by Gardener's Cottage 1
Number One 4
Twenty Princes Street 3

This reputable contemporary art gallery has been exhibiting cutting-edge national and international artists' work since it took over the city's former fruit and veg market building in the 1970s. There's no permanent collection at the **Fruitmarket Gallery**; just a changing series of innovative displays that has previously included work from the late influential sculpture artist Louise Bourgeois and a slightly sinister study of self and symmetry by Mark Wallinger.

Also within the complex is a small bookshop selling art and design titles, as well as an excellent café (see page 82) and, since 2021, a cavernous warehouse hosting music, theatre and club nights.

City Art Centre

MAP PAGE 76
2 Market St. www.edinburghmuseums.org.uk. Free.

Home to probably the most diverse body of post sixteenth-century Scottish art in the world, the **City Art Centre**'s collection represents every national movement from the post-Impressionist Glasgow Boys to the Colourists of the early 1900s. Particularly interesting from a historical perspective is the gallery's scenescape collection of Edinburgh's streets and markets that stretches back as far as the sixteenth century.

The gallery's six floors are also used to display a wide range of temporary exhibits that have included the original Star Wars costumes and a sculpture compilation from the late 70s and 80s.

Princes Street Gardens

MAP PAGE 76
0131 529 7921. Free.

It's hard to imagine that the **Princes Street Gardens**, which flank nearly the entire length of Princes Street, were once the stagnant, foul-

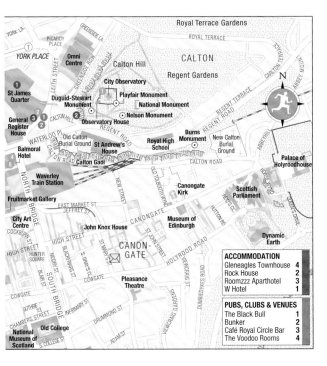

ACCOMMODATION	
Gleneagles Townhouse	4
Rock House	2
Roomzzz Aparthotel	3
W Hotel	1

PUBS, CLUBS & VENUES	
The Black Bull	1
Bunker	2
Café Royal Circle Bar	3
The Voodoo Rooms	4

Scott Monument

smelling Nor' Loch into which the effluent of the Old Town flowed for centuries. The railway has since replaced the water and, today, a sunken cutting carries the main lines out of Waverley Station to the west and north. The gardens, split into east and west sections, were originally the private domain of Princes Street residents and their well-placed acquaintances, only becoming a public park in 1876. These days, the swathes of green lawn, colourful flowerbeds and mature trees are a green lung for the city centre: on sunny days, local office workers appear in their droves at lunchtime, while in the runup to Christmas the gardens' eastern section is home to a German Market, a towering Ferris wheel and other appealingly lit rides. The larger and more verdant western section has the world's first floral clock from 1903 and the Ross Bandstand, a popular but tired-looking Festival venue that is braced for demolition and replacement, with an intriguing earth sheltered structure, fittingly dubbed the "Hobbit-House" for its undulating roof and arched frontage. Cross the

nearby footbridge over the railway tracks and the gardens diverge east towards the lush slopes below the castle's esplanade and west, swinging around the castle's precipitous flank up towards the **Old Town**.

Scott Monument

MAP PAGE 76
East Princes Street Gardens.
www.edinburghmuseums.org.uk. Charge.
Facing the Victorian shopping emporium *Jenners*, and set within East Princes Street Gardens, the 200ft-high **Scott Monument** was erected in memory of prolific author and patriot Sir Walter Scott within a few years of his death. The largest monument in the world to a man of letters, the architecture is closely modelled on Scott's beloved Melrose Abbey (see page 134), and the rich sculptural decoration shows sixteen Scottish writers and sixty-four characters from Scott's famous *Waverley* novels. On the central plinth at the base of the monument is a **statue** of Scott with his deerhound Maida, carved from a 30-ton block of Carrara marble.

Inside, a tightly winding spiral staircase climbs 287 steps to a narrow platform near the top: from here, you can enjoy some inspiring – if vertiginous – vistas of the city below and hills and firths beyond.

National Gallery of Scotland

MAP PAGE 76

The Mound, Princes St. www.national galleries.org. Free; charge for some temporary exhibitions.

Built as a "temple to the fine arts" in 1850, the **National Gallery of Scotland** houses Scotland's premier collection of pre-twentieth-century **European art** in the larger of two grand Neoclassical buildings found at the foot of the Mound.

Though by no means as vast as national collections found elsewhere in Europe, it does include a clutch of exquisite Old Masters and some superb Impressionist works. Benefiting greatly from being a manageable size, its series of elegant octagonal rooms is enlivened by imaginative displays and a pleasantly unrushed atmosphere.

On the ground floor, the rooms have been restored to their 1850s appearance, with pictures hung closely together on claret-coloured walls, often on two levels, and intermingled with sculptures and objets d'art to produce a deliberately cluttered effect. As a result, some lesser works, which would otherwise languish in the vaults, are on display, a good 15ft up. The **layout** is broadly chronological, starting in the upper rooms above the gallery's entrance on the Mound and continuing clockwise around the ground floor.

Among the gallery's most valuable treasures are **Hugo van der Goes'** *Trinity Panels*, on a long-term loan from the Royal Family. Painted in the mid-fifteenth century, they were commissioned by Provost Edward Bonkil for the Holy Trinity Collegiate Church, which was later demolished to make way for Edinburgh's Waverley Station. Bonkil can be seen amid the company of organ-playing angels in the best-preserved of the four panels, while on the reverse sides are portraits of James III, his son (the future James IV) and Queen Margaret of Denmark. The panels are turned by the gallery staff regularly.

Elsewhere, proudly displayed in its own room, Poussin's Seven Sacraments series marks the first attempt to portray scenes from the life of Jesus realistically, rather than through images dictated by artistic conventions.

Among the canvases by **Rembrandt** are a poignant *Self-Portrait Aged 51* and the suggestive *Woman in Bed*, which is thought to represent the biblical figure of Sarah on her wedding night, waiting for her husband Tobias to put the devil to flight.

Among the gallery's Scottish contingent and one of the most popular portraits is the immediately recognizable painting of a lesser-known pastor, *Reverend Robert Walker Skating on Duddingston Loch*, by **Henry Raeburn**.

Royal Scottish Academy

MAP PAGE 76

The Mound. www.royalscottishacademy. org. Free; entrance charge for some temporary exhibitions.

Calton Hill

Gravestones in Old Calton Burial Ground

Based in the impressive Grecian building at the foot of the Mound, the **Royal Scottish Academy** was founded in 1826 as a unique independent body with a remit to promote contemporary Scottish art through exhibitions, scholarship administration and residencies. Its archive of well over a thousand canvases and architectural works stretching back to the eighteenth century is considered a "Recognised Collection of National Significance" by Museum Galleries Scotland.

The exhibitions broadly focus on the modern, however, as the very best of the nation's emerging and established talent get a rare opportunity to display their wares in a prestigious gallery. If you see something you like, it might be possible to take it home. Many of the displays are for sale, though the prices are generally out of reach of most people.

Calton Hill

MAP PAGE 76

Edinburgh's enduring tag as the "Athens of the North" is nowhere better earned than on **Calton Hill**, the volcanic crag that rises above the eastern end of Princes Street. Numerous architects homed in on it as a showcase for their most ambitious and grandiose buildings and monuments. It's also one of the best viewpoints from which to appreciate the cityscape, with its tightly knitted suburbs, landmark Old and New Town buildings and the Firth of Forth beyond.

Calton Gaol

MAP PAGE 76

Waterloo Place. No public access.

Many visitors arriving into Waverley Station at Calton Hill's southern drop imagine the picturesque castellated building pressed hard up against the rock to be Edinburgh Castle itself. In fact, it's the only surviving part of the **Calton Gaol**, once Edinburgh's main prison and where former serial killer William Burke spent his final hours before being executed on Lawnmarket. Most of the prison was demolished in the 1930s to make way for the looming Art Deco St Andrew's House, today occupied by civil servants. The door to the cell of the condemned was reclaimed and can now be seen in the *Beehive Inn* (see page 62).

Old Calton Burial Ground

MAP PAGE 76

Waterloo Place. Free.

On Calton Hill's southern slopes, tucked behind a line of high, dark, forbidding walls, the picturesque assembly of mausoleums and gravestones of **Old Calton Burial Ground**, some at a jaunty angle and others weathered with age, makes for an absorbing wander. Notable among the monuments are the cylindrical memorial by Robert Adam to the philosopher David Hume, one of Edinburgh's greatest sons, and a piercing obelisk commemorating various political martyrs.

Nelson Monument

MAP PAGE 76
Summit of Calton Hill. www.edinburgh museums.org.uk. Charge.

Robert Louis Stevenson reckoned that Calton Hill was the best place to view Edinburgh, "since you can see the Castle, which you lose from the Castle, and Arthur's Seat, which you cannot see from Arthur's Seat". Though the panoramas from ground level are spectacular enough, those from the top of the **Nelson Monument**, perched near the summit of Calton Hill, are even better. Each day at 1pm, a white ball drops down a mast at the top of the monument; this, together with the one o'clock gun fired from the Castle battlements (daily, except Sun), once provided a daily check for the mariners of Leith, who needed accurate chronometers to ensure reliable navigation at sea.

National Monument

MAP PAGE 76
Summit of Calton Hill. Always open.

The **National Monument** is often referred to as "Edinburgh's Disgrace", yet many locals admire this unfinished and somewhat ungainly attempt to replicate the Parthenon atop Calton Hill. Begun in 1826 as a memorial to the victims of the Napoleonic Wars, the project's shortage of funds led architect William Playfair to ensure that even with just twelve of the massive columns completed, the folly would still serve as a striking landmark.

City Observatory

MAP PAGE 76
Summit of Calton Hill. www.collective-edinburgh.art. Free.

Designed by William Playfair in 1818, the **City Observatory** is the largest of the buildings at the summit of Calton Hill although because of pollution and the advent of street lighting, which impaired views of the stars, the observatory proper had to be relocated to Blackford Hill (see page 124) before the end of the nineteenth century. The space is home to the **Collective**, a contemporary art gallery hosting frequent exhibitions as well as workshops, plays, art events and talks from local creatives. On the southwest corner is the castellated Observatory House, one of the few surviving buildings by James Craig, designer of the New Town. Guided tours explore the glorious medley of art, architecture and astronomy, offering a fascinating insight into the history of Calton Hill, the design of the buildings and a behind-the-scenes glimpse into how the observatory was reimagined as a cultural hub (email hires@collective-edinburgh.art for tours).

The National Monument on Calton Hill

Shop

Johnnie Walker Princes Street

MAP PAGE 76
145 Princes St. www.johnniewalker.com.
British booze powerhouse Diageo (behind Guinness and Smirnoff) teamed up with eight Scotch whisky brands in 2019 to open Johnnie Walker Princes Street, a temple to single malt whisky. Spread across an eight-storey Art Deco edifice, the ground-floor shop is filled with limited-edition bottles, sustainable clothing and other gifts; there's even an engraving service. There are whisky tastings in the underground cellar, immersive tours, food and whisky pairings in the *Explorers' Bothy*, and excellent cocktails served with fine views in the *1820 Rooftop Bar*.

Cafés

Milk at the Fruitmarket Gallery

MAP PAGE 76
45 Market St. www.fruitmarket.co.uk.
This attractive café feels like an extension of the gallery space, its airy, reflective ambience enhanced by the wall of glass onto the street. Lots of colourful, modern and healthy brunch options are served here, like avocado and za'atar with poached egg on toast. Artisan cakes and expensive coffee, too. ££

Palm Court

MAP PAGE 76
The Balmoral Hotel, 1 Princes St.
www.roccofortehotels.com.
The ultimate afternoon-tea experience; within the *Balmoral Hotel* complex the oval-shaped *Palm Court*, with its glass cupola, Grecian pillars and tall potted palms, has somehow struck a balance between decadence and tasteful understatement. Try the hotel's signature tea blend with the exquisite handmade pastries while a harpist recites from the balcony. ££££

Restaurants

Contini – The Scottish Café and Restaurant

MAP PAGE 76
National Gallery of Scotland, The Mound.
www.contini.com.
Beneath the National Gallery, *Contini* offers gorgeous views east across Princes Street Gardens and the Old Town. Its fine Scottish cuisine makes it a popular lunchtime target for well-heeled office workers: express lunch menus usually start with soup and finish with a Scottish mainstay like haggis, neeps and tatties. £££

Duck & Waffle

MAP PAGE 76
Entrance on St James Crescent, St James Quarter. www.duckandwaffle.com.
Duck & Waffle opened its first venture outside London in Edinburgh's shiny new shopping complex. Expect playful dishes made from Scottish-sourced ingredients, such as ox cheek, haggis and duck fat caramel served with a dinky pot of Bovril, or the signature crispy duck leg confit topped with a fried duck egg and drizzled with mustard maple syrup. An outdoor terrace takes in fine city views. ££££

The Lookout by Gardener's Cottage

MAP PAGE 76
Calton Hill. www.thelookoutedinburgh.co.
The team behind the New Town's much-loved *Gardener's Cottage* paired up with the Collective (see page 81) to feed hungry patrons visiting the contemporary art centre. Unquestionably Edinburgh's most uniquely located restaurant: atop Calton Hill, its floor-to-ceiling windows oblige vistas across the Forth and, on clear days, as far as

the Trossachs. The restaurant's 42 covers are heavily sought after but book ahead to enjoy home-cooked French-inspired cuisine using predominately Scottish farmed or foraged ingredients. Dishes might include roe deer and hazelnut tagliatelle or salt-baked beetroot with goat's curd. Visit at lunch for the good-value set menu. ££££

Number One

MAP PAGE 76
Balmoral Hotel, 1 Princes St.
www.roccofortehotels.com.
Edinburgh's most reputable and expensive restaurant, set within the *Balmoral Hotel* complex. Opt for the seven-course tasting menu and you can expect a cacophony of colours, foams and flavours to challenge your palate (and your bank balance). ££££

Twenty Princes Street

MAP PAGE 76
First floor, 20 Princes St.
www.twentyprincesstreet.co.uk.
Ambitious fine-dining restaurant specializing in charcoal-grilled meat and game served with exciting accompaniments like smoked shoulder croquette and saffron potato puffs. £££

Pubs, clubs & venues

The Black Bull

MAP PAGE 76
43 Leith St. www.theblackbull-edinburgh.co.uk.
A true veteran, this classic old rock pub has defied the wave of gentrification that has, in recent years, swallowed up most of its contemporaries. Expect a good range of bourbons, a solid jukebox and a lively body of regulars.

Bunker

MAP PAGE 76
2–6 Calton Rd. www.pivo-edinburgh.co.uk.

Palm Court

You might recognize this bar's exterior from the memorable opening sequence of the cult film, *Trainspotting*. The drinking den makes little mention of its famous cameo and instead promotes itself as a Czech beer cellar, live-music venue, and pre- and post-club hangout.

Café Royal Circle Bar

MAP PAGE 76
19 West Register St.
www.caferoyaledinburgh.com.
Worth a visit just for its splendid Victorian decor, notably the huge elliptical island bar and tiled portraits of renowned inventors. Although the pub has a somewhat transient clientele as office workers and well-heeled shoppers duck in and out, the atmosphere here is perfectly genial and conversations are refreshingly audible.

The Voodoo Rooms

MAP PAGE 76
19a West Register St.
www.thevoodoorooms.com.
Glamorous and stylish Victorian bar, dining room and events space that attracts a dressed-up crowd, especially at the weekend. Frequent live music, performance and club nights.

The New Town

The New Town, itself well over two hundred years old, stands in stark contrast to the Old Town: the streets are broad and straight, and most of the buildings are Neoclassical. Originally intended to be residential, the entire area, right down to the names of its streets, is something of a celebration of the Union, which, at the time when building began in 1767, was nevertheless far from universally popular. Today, the main thoroughfares form the bustling hub of the city's commercial, retail and business life, dominated by shops, banks and offices. In many ways, the layout of the greater New Town is its own most remarkable sight, an extraordinary cluster of squares, circuses, terraces, crescents and parks that displays a restrained symmetry. On the ground, many buildings offer a unique twist on the architectural theme, particularly on Queen and George streets, and Charlotte and St Andrew squares.

George Street

MAP PAGE 86

Lined with designer outlets, boutique shops, cocktail bars and flashy restaurants, **George Street**

Melville Monument in St Andrew Square

is by far the most interesting and attractive thoroughfare in the New Town. Most of the original Neoclassical buildings survive, even though their intended purpose as residential housing has long since expired. One original that didn't make it was the old Physician's Hall, demolished early in Victoria's reign to make way for The Dome, a spectacular Greco-Roman building with an ostentatious interior testament to the wealth and power of the bank that made its headquarters there.

Three main thoroughfares cut perpendicularly across George Street – each with an important statue at the intersection; those of Church of Scotland leader, Thomas Chalmers, Prime Minister Pitt the Younger and King George III – and each offers a decent mélange of independent and chain shops, cafés and restaurants.

St Andrew Square

MAP PAGE 86

A bedroom at The Georgian House

Lying at the eastern end of George Street is the smartly landscaped **St Andrew Square**, whose centre is marked by the Melville Monument, a towering column topped by a statue of Lord Melville, Pitt the Younger's Navy Treasurer. Around the edge of the square, you'll find Edinburgh's bus station; the city's swankiest shopping arcade, Multrees Walk; and a handsome eighteenth-century town mansion, designed by Sir William Chambers. Still the ceremonial headquarters of the Royal Bank of Scotland, the palatial mid-nineteenth-century banking hall is a symbol of the success of the New Town.

Charlotte Square

MAP PAGE 86

At the western tip of George Street, Charlotte Square was designed by Robert Adam in 1791, a year before his death. For the most part, his plans were faithfully implemented, an exception being the domed and porticoed church of St George, simplified on grounds of expense. Generally regarded as the epitome of the New Town's elegant simplicity, the square was once the most exclusive residential address in Edinburgh, and though much of it is now occupied by offices, the imperious dignity of the architecture is still clear to see. Indeed, the north side, the finest of Adam's designs, is once again the city's premier postcode, with the official residence of the First Minister of the Scottish Government at no. 6 (Bute House), the Edinburgh equivalent of 10 Downing Street.

Georgian House

MAP PAGE 86

7 Charlotte Sq. www.nts.org.uk. Charge; NTS.

Restored by the National Trust for Scotland, the interior of this residential townhouse provides a revealing sense of well-to-do New Town living in the early nineteenth century. Though a little stuffy and lifeless, the rooms are impressively decked out in period **furniture** – look for the working barrel organ that plays a selection of Scottish airs – and hung with fine **paintings**, including portraits by Scottish artists Sir Henry Raeburn and Allan Ramsay, seventeenth-century Dutch cabinet pictures and the beautiful *Marriage of the Virgin* by El Greco's teacher, the Italian miniaturist Giulio Clovio. In the basement you can see the original wine cellar, lined with roughly made bins, and a **kitchen** complete with an open fire for roasting and a separate oven for baking; video reconstructions of life below and above stairs are shown in a nearby room.

Queen Street

MAP PAGE 86

The last of the New Town's three main streets and the least tarnished by post-Georgian development. **Queen Street**'s southern side is taken over mostly by offices, while across the road there's a huge private residents' garden. There are few individual attractions here, with the exception of the **Scottish National Portrait Gallery** at the eastern end, just to the north of St Andrew Square.

Scottish National Portrait Gallery

MAP PAGE 86

1 Queen St. www.nationalgalleries.org. Free.

Housed in a fantastic Gothic Revivalist palace in red sandstone, the **Scottish National Portrait Gallery** makes an extravagant contrast to the New Town's prevailing Neoclassicism. The exterior of the building is encrusted with statues of national heroes, a theme reiterated in the stunning two-storey entrance hall by William Hole's tapestry-like frieze and mural, carefully restored in the building's revamp.

The gallery's collection extends to over 30,000 images, with seventeen exhibition spaces exploring the differing characteristics of Scotland as a nation and a people. Inevitably, oil paintings of the likes of Mary, Queen of Scots and Robert Burns form the backbone of the curation,

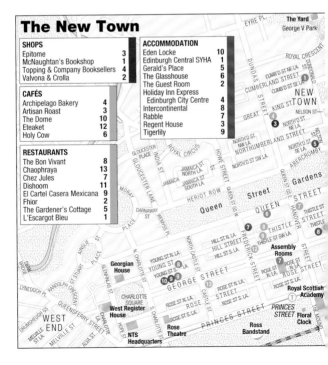

The New Town

SHOPS
Epitome	3
McNaughtan's Bookshop	1
Topping & Company Booksellers	4
Valvona & Crolla	2

CAFÉS
Archipelago Bakery	4
Artisan Roast	3
The Dome	10
Eteaket	12
Holy Cow	6

RESTAURANTS
The Bon Vivant	8
Chaophraya	13
Chez Jules	7
Dishoom	11
El Cartel Casera Mexicana	9
Fhior	2
The Gardener's Cottage	5
L'Escargot Bleu	1

ACCOMMODATION
Eden Locke	10
Edinburgh Central SYHA	1
Gerald's Place	5
The Glasshouse	6
The Guest Room	2
Holiday Inn Express Edinburgh City Centre	4
Intercontinental	8
Rabble	7
Regent House	3
Tigerlily	9

Edinburgh's art scene

With a backdrop as aesthetic as Edinburgh's, it's little wonder that the city's art scene thrives not only in the main galleries, but also on the streets through outdoor markets and in independent outlets.

If your visit to Edinburgh coincides with the end of the academic year, then the huge Degree Show at the prestigious College of Art is well worth a good couple of hours' perusal. Just prior to this is the **Hidden Door** alternative arts festival, a volunteer-run bonanza of visual art installations, music and various other creative outlets.

For exhibitions by established artists, the best place to go is Dundas Street in the New Town where you'll find a cluster of reputable independent galleries within feet of one another.

EDINBURGH COLLEGE OF ART

74 Lauriston Place. www.eca.ed.ac.uk. Free.

An increasingly popular event on the art calendar, the Degree Show attracts private collectors and gallery owners hoping to scout out the best of this year's crop of graduating students. The output on display is always diverse and on the whole – for better or worse – much bolder than you would find in a commercial gallery.

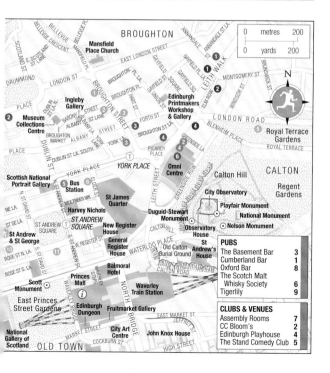

PUBS

The Basement Bar	3
Cumberland Bar	1
Oxford Bar	8
The Scotch Malt Whisky Society	6
Tigerlily	9

CLUBS & VENUES

Assembly Rooms	7
CC Bloom's	2
Edinburgh Playhouse	4
The Stand Comedy Club	5

but there's a lot to be said for the contemporary portraits that often show a country in cultural flux. One such exhibition showed Scottish photographer Graham MacIndoe's own harrowing descent into heroin addiction, a scourge that was at epidemic levels in the housing schemes of Leith in the late 80s.

Beyond the collection and exhibitions, the gallery organizes tours, art classes and even the occasional harp recital.

Broughton Street

MAP PAGE 86

Over the years, this short stretch of New Town tarmac has transformed into a foodie hotspot, with a combination of faddish bars and diners, traditional Victorian boozers and fine-dining restaurants. It all stemmed from the opening of Real Foods, an organic supermarket in the mid-70s that drew in punters from across the city and beyond. More innovators have since moved in, including Artisan Roast which was at the helm of the coffee revolution, sourcing and roasting its own beans before it was all the rage.

It's not just cafés and restaurants here, however, boutique shops fill the gaps with artisan produce on sale, from clothes to Scandinavian haberdashery.

Ingleby Gallery

MAP PAGE 86

33 Barony St. www.inglebygallery.com. Set unexpectedly among the residential houses of this cobbled Georgian street to the northwest of Calton Hill, the **Ingleby Gallery** is a highly reputable exhibition space that attracts the work of little-known artists from around the world. Recent displays have included eccentric Antiguan painter,

The gardens of the New Town

Designed to relieve the wanton overcrowding of Edinburgh's medieval Old Town that had left the city in the grip of the mid-seventeenth-century plague, James Craig's New Town design was deliberately spacious, balancing wide boulevards, attractive squares and mansion houses with, revolutionarily, huge communal parkland. The pungent Nor' Loch that had for centuries absorbed the city's effluent was drained to produce Princes Street Gardens. To the north of the original New Town at Queen Street, a similar near-symmetrical garden was created.

It was a popular idea and when further proposals to expand the New Town to the north, east and west from the 1800s were put together, gardens played a fundamental role in the designs. Many were small and squeezed into residential crescents or squares; others were enormous and set in beautiful and dramatic scenery. The forested Dean Gardens, just downstream from Dean Village (see page 96) on the Water of Leith, for example, has breathtaking views onto Dean Bridge, St Bernard's Well and a mighty waterfall. Regent Gardens, largest private park in town is draped across a huge tranche of Calton hill and has tennis courts, a putting green and a ha-ha.

Visiting the gardens can be problematic because, with the exception of Princes Street Gardens and St Andrew Square, most are privately owned by local residents. Occasional open days are announced, and gardens sometimes open their gates during the Open Doors weekend (www.doorsopendays.org.uk) in September.

sculptor and writer Frank Walter, whose works have included Hitler playing cricket and Charles and Diana portrayed as Adam and Eve.

Mansfield Place Church

MAP PAGE 86
Mansfield Place. www.mansfieldtraquair. org.uk.

The highlight of the Broughton Street area is the neo-Norman **Mansfield Place Church**. It shelters a cycle of murals by the Dublin-born Phoebe Anna Traquair, a leading light in the Scottish Arts and Crafts movement. Covering vast areas of the walls and ceilings of the main nave and side chapels, the wonderfully luminous paintings depict biblical parables and texts, with rows of angels, cherubs flecked with gold, and worshipping figures painted in delicate pastel colours.

Museum Collections Centre

MAP PAGE 86
10 Broughton Market. www.edinburgh museums.org.uk. Free, booking essential.

One of a pair of warehouses in the city, the **Museum Collections Centre** in Broughton Market (along with its sister depository in Granton) holds the reserve collections for Edinburgh's main museums. Uniquely, and unbeknownst to most locals, both open their doors to the public for guided tours. Naturally, the experience is very different to a normal museum; artefacts are racked tightly together and there are no item descriptions or expensive cafés here, but you do get a sense of privilege being able to have a good nose around.

The collection is particularly focussed on Edinburgh's own heritage, displaying artefacts through the centuries that were either made in the city or used there. More recent items like Chopper bikes or shop signs rub shoulders with the original

Edinburgh Printmakers

model for the Scott Monument, cannonballs and even bags of archaeological soil.

With around 130,000 items held here, it's impossible to see it all, but if you have a particular area of interest you can book a free tailored tour.

Edinburgh Printmakers Workshop and Gallery

MAP PAGE 86
23 Union St. www.edinburghprintmakers. co.uk. Free.

Established in the late 1960s as the first open-access studio in Scotland, the **Edinburgh Printmakers Workshop and Gallery** provides the opportunity for artists to engage in the practice of fine art printmaking, including etching, lithography and digital. Visitors can peer down at the artists at work from a balcony or even get involved themselves by signing up to one of the courses offered here. Exhibitions are always running, too – which are free to enter – and there's a decent shop where you can pick up prints and gifts on the way out.

Topping & Company Booksellers

Shops

Epitome

MAP PAGE 86
35 Dundas St. www.epitomeof
edinburgh.com.
Polished but not pretentious, Epitome stocks cool fashion labels from around the world – think A.P.C and Girls of Dust – as well as curated homeware and skincare icons like Haeckels. Look out for the butter-soft cashmere from the owner's own brand, Cameron Taylor.

McNaughtan's Bookshop

MAP PAGE 86
3a–4a Haddington Place, Leith Walk.
www.mcnaughtans.co.uk.
Probably Edinburgh's oldest purveyor of antiquarian literature. Housed in a beautiful old basement, there's also a contemporary art exhibition space.

Topping & Company Booksellers

MAP PAGE 86
2 Blenheim Place. www.toppingbooks.
co.uk.
Opened in 2019, Topping & Company is a welcome addition to the New Town: a huge independent bookstore with over 70,000 books arranged on handcrafted shelves – and, thankfully, library ladders to access them.

Valvona & Crolla

MAP PAGE 86
19 Elm Row, Leith Walk.
www.valvonacrolla.co.uk.
Edinburgh's oldest and most venerated deli, with Italian market produce personally imported weekly from Milan.

Cafés

Archipelago Bakery

MAP PAGE 86
39 Dundas St. www.archipelagobakery.
co.uk.
Serving up some of Edinburgh's crustiest loaves, this sweet-scented bakery is the place to sit and drink coffee while marvelling at the mouth-watering breads, pies and pastries thrust out of the ovens before you. £

Artisan Roast

MAP PAGE 86
57 Broughton St. www.artisanroast.co.uk.
A seemingly unstoppable force in the connoisseur coffee-roasters' market, *Artisan Roast* is behind the sweet, nutty brews found in independent cafés all over town, but to see where the revolution started, head to this narrow, grungy shop with hessian beans bags for decor. £

The Dome

MAP PAGE 86
14 George St. www.thedomeedinburgh.
com.
Ludicrously opulent, this early Victorian complex of cafés, restaurants and bars is a feast for the eyes. It's an unashamed melange of Corinthian columns, marbled floors and chandeliers, topped off

with a huge glass dome. Afternoon tea is a highlight here. £££

Eteaket

MAP PAGE 86

41a Frederick St. www.eteaket.co.uk.
The best of the tea boutiques in the city centre, with restrained but contemporary decor and tables spilling onto the pavement outside. Order from its huge range of loose teas – perhaps the award-winning silver needle (a white tea) – and you'll be served a petite pot alongside a timer so you know exactly when to end the steeping process. ££

Holy Cow

MAP PAGE 86

34 Elder St. www.bit.ly/holycowed.
Bright, friendly vegan café that specializes in mini 'Muu burgers', egg-free cakes and dairy-free lattes. The plant-based burgers, served with a sizeable portion of chips, come in a range of forms like hoisin-marinated tofu or pulled jackfruit. ££

Restaurants

The Bon Vivant

MAP PAGE 86

55 Thistle St. www.bonvivantedinburgh.co.uk.
The New Town's hottest hangout sees expert mixologists whip up citrus-spiked Gin Fizzes and velvety Negronis from behind a wood-clad bar. Post-cocktail, diners mooch into the adjoining restaurant to feast on traditional Scottish plates with a modern twist – haggis bon bons followed by pan-fried hake or slow-roasted pork belly. £££

Chaophraya

MAP PAGE 86

4th floor, 33 Castle St. www.chaophraya.co.uk.
Thai rooftop restaurant with a "Glassbox" section offering a near 360-degree view of the city. The menu is stunning too; reasonably priced and packed with interesting seafood choices like red-curry battered prawns and sweet-and-sour red snapper. £££

Chez Jules

MAP PAGE 86

109 Hanover St. www.chezjulesbistro.com.
Run by the former boss of the once-mighty *Pierre Victoire* bistro chain. The formula is much the same: cheap and generous set menus, good table wine and an informal setting. Your two-course lunch might include French onion soup and coq au vin with mash. £££

Dishoom

MAP PAGE 86

3a St Andrew Square. www.dishoom.com.
Recreating all the trappings of Old Bombay's Persian cafés; all that's missing is the sweat dripping off your chin. Diners receive an effusive welcome followed by the patience-of-an-Indian-saint waiting staff as you endeavour to comprehend the extensive menu. Pick the Pau Bhaji – curry and a home-made roll – and the devilishly smoky gunpowder potatoes, and you'll be off to a flying start. £££

El Cartel Casera Mexicana

MAP PAGE 86

64 Thistle St. www.elcartelmexicana.co.uk.
Mexican *antojitos* (tapas-sized street food) served with funky margaritas in a cool setting that draws heavily from the Día de los Muertos festival. Tacos, street corn and quesadillas feature on the menu as well as more unusual plates like crispy ox tongue. £

Fhior

MAP PAGE 86

36 Broughton St. www.fhior.com.
Scandi-chic *Fhior* is the latest venture from chef Scott Smith, formerly of (now closed) *Norn*. Playfulness is at the heart of the culinary experience; diners are encouraged to eat blind to enjoy the food without any preconceptions.

Dishes are rooted in place, drawing on the natural larder of Scotland – think red mullet with leek and mushroom or veal with bone marrow and wild garlic. You do, however, need deep pockets for the privilege: the seven-course tasting is £85; ten courses £105 (double that for drink pairing). ££££

The Gardener's Cottage

MAP PAGE 86
1 Royal Terrace Gardens, London Rd. www.thegardenerscottage.co.

In an achingly beautiful little cottage uniquely situated in a parkland setting, dining is intimate, in two small rooms with communal long tables. Diners get a front-row seat to the culinary theatre in the miniscule open kitchen, where the talented team prepares six outstanding courses of Scottish design (vegetarian option available). ££££

L'Escargot Bleu

MAP PAGE 86
56 Broughton St. www.lescargotbleu.co.uk.
A big step on from the rustic, no-frills French bistro of yesteryear, here classic French country cooking is brought to bear on

L'Escargot Bleu

locally sourced produce – with an occasional Scottish twist, as in the moules marinières cullen skink style. Two-course lunch and pre-theatre menus are a snip. ££££

Pubs

The Basement Bar

MAP PAGE 86
10a–12a Broughton St. www.basement-bar-edinburgh.co.uk.

Mexican cantina and cocktail bar that celebrates everything about Mexico that's cool, from the Día de Muertos decor to the reputable kitchen that's been churning out top-notch burritos, fajitas and tortillas for over two decades. For those who love spicy food, the Firecracker Tacos with fried broccoli, smoked almond and habanero puree has a mighty kick, especially when drizzled with the accompanying bottle of house chipotle.

Cumberland Bar

MAP PAGE 86
1–3 Cumberland St. www.cumberlandbar.co.uk.

This lovely old pub is just far enough off the beaten track to dodge the weekend's pub-crawling masses. Its other great assets are its willow-shaded beer garden and fantastic assortment of cask ales.

Oxford Bar

MAP PAGE 86
8 Young St. 0131 539 7119.

Unpretentious, unspoilt, no-nonsense city bar – which is why local crime writer Ian Rankin and his Inspector Rebus like it so much. Fans duly make the pilgrimage, but fortunately not all the regulars have been scared off.

The Scotch Malt Whisky Society

MAP PAGE 86
28 Queen St. www.smws.com.

An essential stop for whisky aficionados, with regular guest

Assembly Rooms

speakers and sampling sessions plus a public bar with over 200 malts and paired real ale chasers. Three of the grand Georgian buildings' four floors are reserved for members but the ground-floor *Kaleidoscope* bar is open to all and serves hearty Scottish bar food.

Tigerlily

MAP PAGE 86
125 George St. www.tigerlilyedinburgh. co.uk.
The poster child of all George Street's decadent destination bars, where the locals come to see and be seen. Partitioned into various lounges, each with its own boutique personality, *Tigerlily* manages to retain an intimate vibe despite the raucous hen parties and cocktail-fuelled dance-floor posturing.

Clubs and venues

Assembly Rooms

MAP PAGE 86
54 George St. www.assemblyrooms edinburgh.co.uk.
This complex of small and large halls is used all year, but really comes into its own during the Fringe, featuring large-scale drama productions and mainstream comedy.

CC Bloom's

MAP PAGE 86
23–24 Greenside Place.
www.ccblooms.co.uk.
Edinburgh's most enduring gay bar, with a big dancefloor, stonking rhythms, a young, friendly crowd and free entry all night.

Edinburgh Playhouse

MAP PAGE 86
18–22 Greenside Place.
www.playhousetheatre.com.
The largest theatre in Britain with a 3000-plus capacity, the Playhouse is used largely for extended runs of popular musicals and occasional music concerts.

The Stand Comedy Club

MAP PAGE 86
5 York Place. 0131 558 7272.
The city's undisputed comedy heavyweight, with different acts on every night and some of the UK's top comics headlining at the weekends. Be sure to arrive early to secure a good table for the evening.

West End and Dean Village

Much of Edinburgh's wealth is concentrated in its West End, where embassies and lawyers occupy many of the huge Georgian townhouses west of Charlotte Square. On the main thoroughfares and in the pretty cobbled lanes of West End Village, attractive pubs, cafés and restaurants thrive on the affluent footfall from locals and office workers. Further prosperity can be found nearby; Edinburgh's theatre and financial districts in the area south of Princes Street's western tip have seen major developments in recent times, and gentrification has followed suit. On the West End's northern fringe, the gradient drops sharply towards the Water of Leith, where the old milling settlement of Dean Village is an unexpected delight and a good place to begin exploring the city's less touristic treasures.

St Mary's Cathedral

MAP PAGE 96
Palmerston Place. www.cathedral.net.
Free; charge for some guest performances.

With its trio of soaring spires, **St Mary's Cathedral** stabs deep into the city's western horizon. On closer inspection, the cathedral

St Mary's Cathedral

is no less impressive. Entering through its ornamental Gothic portal, your eye is immediately drawn ahead to the stained-glass window triplet above the raised altar. The high vault, supported by a run of symmetrical Gothic arches, gives the place uniquely rich acoustics – best witnessed during Evensong, performed most days by the Cathedral Choir. Lunchtime chamber concerts are also a regular feature here, as are guest choirs and organist performances.

West End Village

MAP PAGE 96

The name "**West End Village**" is a recent concoction, coined to market the unspoiled Georgian shopping lanes of William Street. A popular filming location thanks to its cobbles, Victorian streetlamps and shop frontages – punctuated with original cast-iron balconies – it's a charming area for a short stroll and a cappuccino away from the hustle of the city centre. There is a handful of nice pubs, one (*The Melville*) with tables outside where you can sink a cold one while watching the city's

Usher Hall in Edinburgh's Theatre District

elite swan in and out of the street's boutique shops and beauty salons.

Edinburgh Gin

MAP PAGE 96

1a Rutland Square. www.edinburghgin. com. Charge for tours, advance booking essential.

Right in step with current drinking trends, **Edinburgh Gin** is a small independent distiller that takes pride in the city's 300-year gin production heritage. An array of tours are offered where you can see the beautiful copper stills in action, learn about the production techniques and recipes and perhaps experience a tutored tasting session.

Theatre District

MAP PAGE 96

With highbrow theatres rubbing shoulders with notorious late bars, Edinburgh's **Theatre District**, located on and around Lothian Road, has always had a Jekyll and Hyde reputation. But these days, more than a whiff of gentrification hangs in the air. Modern bars and contemporary kitchens – as they like to be known – are opening in every nip and tuck of the city,

competing with the old Italian stalwarts that have been knocking out pizzas late into the night for generations. The draw, of course, are the theatres themselves, and most attractive of the bunch is the Edwardian Usher Hall. Sandwiched between the Georgian Lyceum and the tiny Traverse theatres, it was built in the Classical style barely seen since Queen Vic was a child and similar in shape, if not size, to London's Royal Albert Hall. A little further south, look out for the vast complex housing the Odeon cinema, one of only a handful of Art Deco buildings in town.

Edinburgh Farmers' Market

MAP PAGE 96

Castle Terrace. Sat 9am–2pm.

Round the back of the Usher Hall, the wide pavements of Castle Terrace with its towering backdrop of the castle provide a convivial setting for the **Edinburgh Farmers' Market**. Unlike the city's other producers' markets, the focus here is more on groceries than street food although you can still get a coffee and a cake and, if you're lucky, a seat.

Dean Village

Dean Village

MAP PAGE 96

Less than half a mile from Princes Street's western end, the old milling community of **Dean Village** is one of central Edinburgh's most picturesque yet unexpected corners, its atmosphere of decay arrested by the conversion of numerous granaries and tall mill buildings into designer flats. Nestling close to the river, with steep banks looming on both sides, the ancient settlement dates back at least as far as the twelfth century. Developed in isolation, the village's warren of lanes and footpaths weaves through a unique assortment of architectural styles, from rubble-stone cottages and mews houses to the ambitious Well Court; a colossal social housing complex that closely resembles a Victorian mansion. The village is bookended by beautiful waterfalls, and glorious walks can be enjoyed in either direction along the Water of Leith.

Dean Bridge

MAP PAGE 96

High above Dean Village, **Dean Bridge**, a bravura feat of 1830s

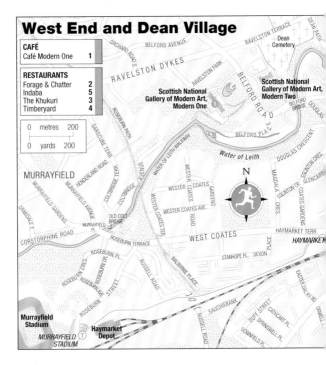

West End and Dean Village

CAFÉ	
Café Modern One	1

RESTAURANTS	
Forage & Chatter	2
Indaba	5
The Khukuri	3
Timberyard	4

0 metres	200
0 yards	200

ORCHARD ROAD S.   BELFORD AVENUE   RAVELSTON TERRACE   DEAN PATH

Dean Cemetery

RAVELSTON PARK

RAVELSTON DYKES

Scottish National Gallery of Modern Art, Modern One

BELFORD ROAD

Scottish National Gallery of Modern Art, Modern Two

BELFORD BRIDGE   DOUGLAS

ROSEBURN PATH

GARSCUBE TERR.

BELFORD PLACE

Water of Leith

WATER OF LEITH WALKWAY

DOUGLAS CRESCENT

N

MURRAYFIELD

HENDERSON ROAD

MURRAYFIELD AVENUE

COLTBRIDGE TERR.

COLTBRIDGE AVENUE

WESTER COATES GARDENS

WESTER COATES

DOUGLAS CRESCENT

MAGDALA CRES.

EGLINTON CR. GLENCAIRN

EGLINTON CRES.

COATES GARDENS

DRUMDRYAN

MURRAYFIELD GARDENS

MURRAYFIELD PL.

OLD COLT BRIDGE

WESTER COATES TER.

WESTER COATES AVE.

WEST COATES

CRES.

HAYMARKET TERR.

CORSTORPHINE ROAD

ROSEBURN TERRACE

BALBIRNIE PLACE

STANHOPE ST   DEVON

HAYMARKET

ROSEBURN CRES.

ROSEBURN PL.

ROSEBURN AVE.

ROSEBURN STREET

RUSSELL ROAD

SAUGHTONBANK

DUFF STREET   CATHCART PL.

EASTER DALRY RD.

SPRINGWELL PL.

Murrayfield Stadium

MURRAYFIELD STADIUM

Haymarket Depot

RUSSELL ROAD

SAUCHIEBANK

DOWNFIELD PL.

engineering by Thomas Telford, carries the main road over 100ft above the river. It marks one of the world's first village bypasses, meaning townsfolk and traders no longer needed to enter Dean village when travelling between Edinburgh and Queensferry. Consequently, its construction marked a steep decline in the prosperity of the village, only arrested in recent decades as the settlement's mills were converted into residential housing.

Scottish National Gallery of Modern Art

MAP PAGE 96

75 Belford Rd. www.nationalgalleries.org. Free; charge for some temporary exhibitions. A free bus service connects the National Gallery of Scotland with the Modern One and Two galleries.

The first collection in Britain devoted solely to post-1800s painting and sculpture is housed across a pair of distinctive Neoclassical buildings, **Modern One** and **Modern Two**. Its grounds serve as a **sculpture park**, featuring works by, among others, Charles Jencks, whose prize-winning *Landform*, a swirling mix of ponds and grassy mounds, dominates the area in front of Modern One.

The art collection here has a strong Scottish contingent, with a particularly fine body of works from the early twentieth-century **Colourists**. The collection's **international paintings** feature crowd-pleasers like Matisse and Picasso, while Hockney, Warhol and Freud form the backbone of a solid post-War catalogue.

The work of Edinburgh-born sculptor **Sir Eduardo Paolozzi**, described by some as the father of Pop Art, features comprehensively in Modern Two. To the right of the main entrance, his London studio has been expertly recreated, right down to the clutter of half-finished casts, toys and empty pots of glue.

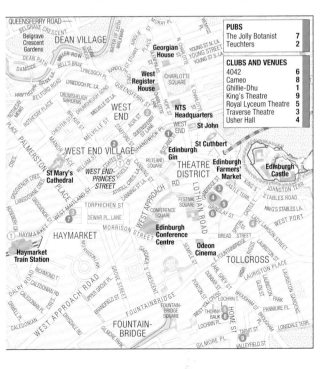

Café

Café Modern One

MAP PAGE 96

Scottish National Gallery of Modern Art, 75 Belford Rd. www.heritageportfolio.co.uk.
One of the nicest cafés in Edinburgh thanks to its delightful walled garden round the back of the Modern One gallery. The canteen here serves up superb healthy lunches, including a range of vibrant home-made salads; three per person should suffice for under a tenner. ££

Restaurants

Forage & Chatter

MAP PAGE 96

1A Alva St. www.forageandchatter.com.
Showcasing the best produce sourced within a 25-mile radius, this concept restaurant garners more accolades these days than any other in town. The distance limitation doesn't seem to affect the offerings here, which regularly include the bounty of the North Sea and field-to-fork ingredients from the city's fringe hill farms. Think confit duck leg with a coffee sauce and scattering of almonds, followed by North Sea pollock and monkfish tail with *pomme mousseline* and rainbow kale. ££££

Indaba

MAP PAGE 96

3 Lochrin Terrace. www.edindaba.co.uk.
An unlikely combination of Scottish, South African and northern Spanish culinary influences, this modest restaurant delivers some interesting tapas. The African contributions are predominantly meaty, like boerewors sausage with chakalaka, while the Spanish plates are typically vibrant and colourful. ££££

The Khukuri

MAP PAGE 96

8 West Maitland St. www.thekhukuri.com.
A slice of Nepal in Scotland, this unassuming diner conjures up culinary flashbacks of the proprietor's childhood in Kathmandu. Starters like momo (dumplings) and pani puri (stuffed and deep-fried crispy crepe) offer a glimpse into Nepalese street food while the curries rely on flavoursome regional herbs and spices like jimbu and timur peppercorns. ££

Timberyard

MAP PAGE 96

10 Lady Lawson St. www.timberyard.co.
With paint-washed brick walls and dark wood accents, this moodily lit restaurant in a converted warehouse is making waves on the restaurant scene for its boundary-pushing cuisine. Simple, seasonal ingredients from local growers are given a Nordic spin – think caramelized pork belly served alongside a heap of buttery cabbage, kimchi and salted apple. Pickling, curing and foraging are all part and parcel of the farm-to-fork process here, and the result has paid off – the kitchen scooped a much-deserved Michelin star. ££££

Pubs

The Jolly Botanist

MAP PAGE 96

256–260 Morrison St. www.thejolly botanist.co.uk.
Riding on the back of gin drinking's phenomenal comeback, this bar has made a name for itself for its range of eclectic spirits sourced from micro-distilleries around the globe.

Teuchters

MAP PAGE 96

26 William St. www.teuchtersbar.co.uk.
The more traditional of the three-pub cluster in William Street and, at times, the liveliest. It's a free house with a good range of Scottish cask ales and plenty of pub grub choices to suit all budgets.

Clubs and venues

4042

MAP PAGE 96

40–42 Grindlay St. www.4042.co.uk.
Small hip-hop and R&B joint
popular with students for its
laidback atmosphere and free-to-
use ping-pong tables.

Cameo

MAP PAGE 96

38 Home St, Tollcross. www.picture
houses.com.
A treasure of an art-house cinema
with a cosy wee bar – opened by
Sean Connery – attached; screens
more challenging mainstream
releases and cult late-nighters.

Ghillie-Dhu

MAP PAGE 96

2 Rutland Place. www.ghillie-dhu.co.uk.
Housed in a rather fancy
auditorium, *Ghillie-Dhu*
wholeheartedly embraces Scotland's
traditional musical heritage. A
rotation of accomplished folk
groups plays throughout the week
(free entry), culminating in Friday
and Saturday's jovial ceilidh nights
(charge).

King's Theatre

MAP PAGE 96

2 Leven St. www.capitaltheatres.com/
your-visit/kings-theatre.
Edwardian civic theatre majoring
in pantomime, touring West End
plays and the occasional drama or
opera performance. The interior is
surprisingly luxurious, with marble
staircases, carved mahogany doors
and a sumptuously regal auditorium.

Royal Lyceum Theatre

MAP PAGE 96

30 Grindlay St. www.lyceum.org.uk.
A fine Victorian civic theatre and
leading venue for mainstream
drama. The theatre commissions
around seven plays annually as well
as hosting travelling productions.

Traverse Theatre

MAP PAGE 96

10 Cambridge St, Lothian Rd.
www.traverse.co.uk.
One of Britain's premier venues for
new plays and avant-garde drama
from around the world. Also has a
lively and popular bar.

Usher Hall

MAP PAGE 96

Lothian Rd. www.usherhall.co.uk.
Edinburgh's main civic concert
hall frequently features choral
and symphony concerts, as well
as legends of country, jazz, world
and pop.

Timberyard

Stockbridge

Between the New Town and the Botanic Gardens, the busy suburb of Stockbridge grew up around the Water of Leith ford and its seventeenth-century bridge, over which cattle were driven to market in Edinburgh. The hamlet was essentially gobbled up in the expansion of the New Town, but a few charming buildings and an independent character prevail in the district today. The area is a popular quarter for young professionals who can't afford the property prices in the New Town proper, and as a result there's a good crop of bars, boutiques and places to eat along both Raeburn Place, the main road, and St Stephen Street, one of Edinburgh's more maverick side streets.

St Stephen Street

MAP PAGE 102

Hosting some of the capital's more eccentric retailers perched above alluring basement restaurants and bars, **St Stephen Street** reveals the bohemian alter-ego to fashionable Stockbridge. Art lovers can peruse petite galleries, while yesteryear is celebrated in antique shops, a vinyl record seller and a couple of vintage fashion emporiums. The street's prosperity may be clear for all to see, but many residents can remember when this swanky corner of Georgian Edinburgh was but a slum. How times have changed.

Stockbridge Market

MAP PAGE 102

Kerr St. www.stockbridgemarket.com. Sun 10am–4pm.

Food stalls at Stockbridge Market

Water of Leith

MAP PAGE 102

Slicing a diagonal cleft from the Pentland hills southwest of town, the Water of Leith twists and churns its peaty, golden-brown burden towards the Shore, Leith's (and now Edinburgh's) attractive old harbour. En route, although comfortably bypassing the city's Old Town, the river trundles by old villages that once depended on its power to drive mills. Nature abounds on this eminently walkable route towards the sea; swans and mallards are commonly seen under the canapé, while otters, mink, dippers and kingfishers make sporadic appearances. Look out for the satellite attractions of the Modern Art Gallery (see page 97) at Dean Village, and the Royal Botanic Gardens (see page 102) near Stockbridge make another good draw from the river's edge. Downstream, the waterway's final twist opens wide at the Shore (see page 112) as the restaurants of the city's gourmet heart swim into view.

A consistently popular street-food destination, **Stockbridge Market** offers a bounty of artisan produce to eat on the hoof or take away. It's a compact affair, sited beneath a grove of leaning Sorbus trees by the banks of the Water of Leith, where the tightly packed stallholders supply a veritable feast for the senses. Even with the belligerent Scottish climate, there's somehow an international buzz as scores of foodies beeline for *Casa Roble*'s excellent paella or *Harajuku Japanese Kitchen*'s udon noodles.

The Yard

MAP PAGE 102

22 Eyre Place Lane. www.theyardscotland. org.uk. Charge for children, adults free. One for the kids, **The Yard** is an exciting, bespoke adventure playground and activity centre designed by team behind the BBC's *DIY SOS* programme. Geared towards children under 11, the focus here is on play how it used to be, with rope swings, roller skates, go-carts, chopper bikes and plenty of hiding places, while indoors there's an art room, books, instruments and a help-yourself café. A welcome and pleasingly anarchic antidote to the sterile, soft play proliferation of recent years.

Fettes College

MAP PAGE 102

Regularly described as the "Eton of the North", and just like its southern rival, **Fettes College** proved it could also churn out prime ministerial material. Perhaps understandably, the school takes no credit for Tony Blair's achievements; one former teacher quipped that he was "the most difficult boy I ever had to deal with".

Another famous ex-pupil, in a fictional sense at least, was James Bond. Fleming had the agent board there for his teens as part of the *You Only Live Twice* backstory. Even Harry Potter can lay a claim to the school which, together with another of Edinburgh's private institutions (George Heriot's), inspired the concept of Hogwarts. Looking at the building, it's not difficult to see why; its dramatic and unique hybridization of French chateaux and the Scots Baronial style is an awe-inspiring sight, particularly when viewed from afar with its central tower thrusting out of the surrounding canopy.

good place for a gentle stroll, with the magnificent backdrop of old Edinburgh at arm's length.

Originally laid out in 1889, much of the grounds is set aside for rugby pitches threaded by tree-lined walkways, while at the eastern fringe, free tennis and basketball/football courts are lined up next to a petanque club and playground. There are also some attractive hidden corners to wander through. The lower part, for instance, has a large boating pond, home to many wildfowl thanks to the reed marsh at one end. Across the path is the sundial garden, a delightful enclosed space with a centerpiece stone sundial from 1890.

Inverleith Park

Inverleith Park

MAP PAGE 102

One of Scotland's largest urban gardens, **Inverleith Park** is a

Royal Botanic Garden

MAP PAGE 102

Arboretum Place. www.rbge.org.uk. Garden free; charge for glasshouses and guided tours.

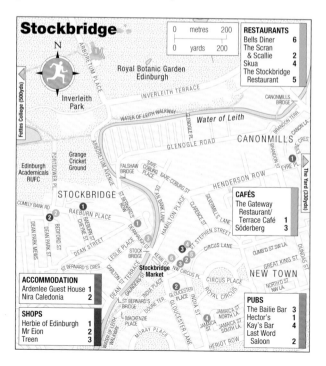

Stockbridge

N

| 0 | metres | 200 |
| 0 | yards | 200 |

RESTAURANTS
Bells Diner 6
The Scran
& Scallie 2
Skua 4
The Stockbridge
Restaurant 5

ARBORETUM ROAD
Fettes College (500yds)
ARBORETUM PLACE
Royal Botanic Garden
Edinburgh
Inverleith
Park
INVERLEITH TERRACE
CANONMILLS
BRIDGE
WATER OF LEITH WALKWAY
Water of Leith
GLENOGLE RD
GLENOGLE ROAD
CANONMILLS
BRANDON TERR.
BRANDON ST
EYRE CRES
EYRE PL
CANON LA.
Grange
Cricket
Ground
ARBORETUM AVENUE
PORTGOWER PL
Edinburgh
Academicals
RUFC
FALSHAW
BRIDGE
SAXE-
COBURG
PLACE
SAXE-COBURG ST
HENDERSON ROW
The Yard (330yds)

CAFÉS
The Gateway
Restaurant/
Terrace Café 1
Söderberg 3

COMELY BANK RD
STOCKBRIDGE
RAEBURN PLACE
CHEYNE ST
ST BERNARD'S ROW
DEAN BANK LANE
HAMILTON PLACE
CLARENCE ST
SILVERMILL'S LANE
ST STEPHEN STREET
CIRCUS LANE
DEAN PARK MEWS
DEAN PARK ST
BEDFORD ST
DEAN STREET
LESLIE PLACE
CARLTON ST
DEANHAUGH ST
STOCK
BRIDGE
KERR ST
NW CIRCUS PL
CIRCUS PLACE
CIRCUS LANE
CUMB'D ST SW LA.
GREAT KING ST
NEW TOWN
DUNDAS ST
CUMB'D ST
NW LA.
NORTH'D ST
NW LA.

ACCOMMODATION
Ardenlee Guest House 1
Nira Caledonia 2

SHOPS
Herbie of Edinburgh 1
Mr Eion 2
Treen 3

ST BERNARD'S CRES
DEAN TERRACE
ST BERNARD'S
BRIDGE
L. ST BERNARD'S
BRIDGE
SAUNDERS ST
INDIA PLACE
DOUNE TERR
GLOUCESTER ST
ROYAL CIRCUS
GLOUCESTER LANE
INDIA ST
JAMICA ST
NORTH LA
JAMICA ST
JAMICA ST
SOUTH LA.
L. MACKENZIE
PLACE
MORAY PLACE
WATER OF LEITH WALKWAY
HERIOT ROW

PUBS
The Bailie Bar 3
Hector's 1
Kay's Bar 4
Last Word
Saloon 2

Stockbridge
Market

Just beyond the northern boundaries of the New Town is the 70-acre site of the **Royal Botanic Garden**. Filled with mature trees and a huge variety of native and exotic plants and flowers, the "Botanics" (as they're commonly called) are most popular simply as a place to stroll and lounge around on the grass. The main entrance is the West Gate on Arboretum Place, through the contemporary, eco-designed John Hope Gateway, where you'll find interpretation areas, information, exhibitions, a shop and restaurant.

The northeastern fringe of the gardens has a series of ten glasshouses including a soaring 1850s Palm House, showing off a steamy array of palms, ferns, orchids, cycads and aquatic plants, including some huge circular water lilies. Pride of the collection in recent years has been the titan arum plant which, around June, produces the world's largest flower. A notoriously stubborn plant to bloom, Edinburgh's specimen has been named Auld Reekie (Edinburgh's nickname)

thanks to its fly-attracting rotting-flesh scent.

Outside, gardens of different themes are highlighted: the large Chinese-style garden, for example, has a bubbling waterfall and the world's largest collection of Asian wild plants outside China, while in the northwest corner there's a Scottish native woodland that effectively evokes the wild unkemptness of parts of the Scottish Highlands and west coast.

Art is a strong theme within the Botanics, with a gallery showing rotating contemporary exhibitions in the attractive eighteenth-century Inverleith House at the centre of the gardens. Scattered all around outdoor sculptures, including a giant pinecone by landscape artist Andy Goldsworthy and the striking stainless-steel east gate, designed in the form of stylized rhododendrons. Parts of the garden are also notable for their great vistas: the lawns near Inverleith House offer one of the city's best views of the Castle and Old Town's steeples and monuments.

The Victorian Palm House at The Royal Botanic Garden

The Scran & Scallie

Shops

Herbie of Edinburgh

MAP PAGE 102
66 Raeburn Place. 0131 332 9888.
Thriving little delicatessen packed from top to toe with everything from gourmet ingredients like wild mushrooms, pickles and pastas to ready-to-eat pies, tortillas and cakes.

Mr Eion

MAP PAGE 102
9 Dean Park St. www.mreion.com.
One for serious coffee drinkers, this small-batch bean roaster sells bags out of its little lab off Stockbridge's main drag. There's a wide selection of single estate beans on sale from around the globe, all with accompanying tasting notes.

Treen

MAP PAGE 102
2–4 St Stephen Place. www.shoptreen.com.
On Edinburgh's prettiest street, Treen is one of a cluster of independent and sustainable shops in this corner of the capital. The vegan fashion store is stocked with a careful curation of clothing – think

brands like Skall Studio and Sancia – along with fragrance products such as divine Earl of East candles and vegan Maya Njie perfumes.

Cafés

The Gateway Restaurant/ Terrace Café

MAP PAGE 102
Royal Botanic Garden, Arboretum Place. www.rbge.org.uk.
At the West Gate of the Botanics, the John Hope Gateway Centre has tables and a terrace overlooking the gardens on its upper floor, serving cream tea as well as full breakfasts and posh lunches made from ingredients grown in the gardens. A few hundred yards beyond, the busy Terrace Café serves coffees, snacks and less formal lunches, with lots of outdoor tables and kid-friendly options. ££

Söderberg

MAP PAGE 102
3 Deanhaugh St. www.soderberg.uk.
Another side to the continental baking scene, this time a Swedish sourdough outfit with some of the finest chewy, crusty loaves in town. It's also a café selling delicate cardamom pastries to go with its satisfyingly nutty coffees. £

Restaurants

Bells Diner

MAP PAGE 102
7 St Stephen St. www.bellsdiner edinburgh.com.
Superb, veteran steak and burger joint that's been knocking out no-nonsense, home-made food since the 70s. The menu is great value, and there is a good range of excellent burgers – beef, chicken, lamb, nut – on the menu. ££

The Scran & Scallie

MAP PAGE 102
1 Comely Bank Rd. www.scranand scallie.com.

With its sister restaurants (*Kitchin* and *Castle Terrace*) vying for fine dining superiority, *Scran & Scallie* sees celebrity chef Tom Kitchin taking on the gastropub market. The food is truly top notch, if a little pricey, with simple but excellent mains including the likes of fish pie and home-made sausage and mash. ££££

Skua

MAP PAGE 102
49 St Stephen St. www.skua.scot.
From the culinary heavyweights behind Michelin-starred *Heron* – uber-chefs Tomás Gormley and Sam Yorke – comes this dinky ten-table basement restaurant flooded with light through its glass facade. The season-driven menu is packed with regularly changing small plates, and might include seabass ceviche, mackerel with baby fennel, or king oyster mushrooms with pickled ginger. ££££

The Stockbridge Restaurant

MAP PAGE 102
54 St Stephen St. www.thestockbridge restaurant.co.uk.
Basement restaurant with fine linen, silverware set alongside blackened stone walls, and a candlelit hearth. The food here is vibrant, made up of numerous beautifully partnered elements like the salmon with crispy squid, roast beetroot and chorizo. Minimum two courses. ££££

Pubs

The Bailie Bar

MAP PAGE 102
2–4 St Stephen St. www.thebailiebar.co.uk.
Frothy cask ales in unpretentious and often rowdy surroundings, *The Bailie* is a traditional pub that's been around long enough to remember when this swanky corner of Georgian Edinburgh was but a slum.

Hector's

MAP PAGE 102
47–49 Deanhaugh St. www.hectors stockbridge.co.uk.
The number-one watering hole in Stockbridge for young professionals, *Hector's* is a spacious but intimate bar with good wines, craft IPA and a popular bar menu with mains like aubergine and falafel burger or chicken, mushroom, pancetta and leek pie.

Kay's Bar

MAP PAGE 102
39 Jamaica St. www.kaysbar.co.uk.
Tucked away in a New Town side street, this former Georgian coaching house was remodelled in the Victorian era as a wine and spirit merchant. Thankfully, it has retained its Victorian charm and now operates as a cosy little pub serving real ale and plenty of whiskies.

Last Word Saloon

MAP PAGE 102
44 St Stephen St. www.lastwordsaloon.com.
Shadowy candlelit bar with open fires and table service, where an abundance of imaginative home-made cocktails forms the backbone of the drinks menu.

Kay's Bar

Leith

Uber-cool Leith, Edinburgh's beating hipster heart, is a hub of creativity with its own distinct arts and music culture and cutting-edge dining scene. It has developed independently of the city up the hill, its history bound up in the hard graft of fishing, shipbuilding and trade. The presence of sailors and merchants has also historically given the place a cosmopolitan – if slightly gritty – edge, still obvious today. Leith's initial revival from down-and-out port to happening waterfront destination began in the 1980s around The Shore, the old harbour at the mouth of the Water of Leith. In recent years, the massive dock areas beyond have been transformed at a rate of knots, with landmark developments including Ocean Terminal, a shopping and entertainment complex, beside which the *Royal Yacht Britannia* is living out her retirement years.

Leith Links

MAP PAGE 108

As its name would suggest, **Leith Links** has a historical golfing affiliation; in fact, it was here that the first official rules that led to the modern game were developed in 1744. The sport was banned a few years after the links were formalized as a park in 1888 and, today, it's an attractive 46-acre public space with tennis courts, bowling greens, a cricket club and community allotments. The perimeter and pathways, interestingly, host one of the largest collections of mature elm trees in the country that are yet to succumb to Dutch Elm disease, wrapping around lawns that are completely flat except for a pair of unexpected hillocks. These are actually two of the remaining artillery mounds from the 1560 Siege of Leith – a standoff between the French and English armies.

Aerial view of Leith Links

The Banana Flats

Just a couple of blocks away from Leith's picturesque old harbour, Cables Wynd House (aka the **Banana Flats**) is arguably one of the most depressing examples of early 1960s **Brutalist** architecture in the country. Built to relieve overcrowding in the nearby tenements, the ten-storey wall of curved (hence its nickname) concrete and prison-barred balconies is an unforgiving vision of apocalyptic decay.

Its low point came during the 80s when the flats became a focal point for Edinburgh's heroin epidemic, though things had improved by the time the building was used as a location in the hit film *Trainspotting*.

Talk of demolishing the flats was on the cards for years until a controversial 2017 decision awarded the building **grade A listed status** – the same protection given to **Edinburgh Castle**.

Trinity House

MAP PAGE 108

99 Kirkgate. 0131 554 3289. Free; HES.

Small appointment-only nautical museum housed in an attractive former guild hall, **Trinity House** possesses a decent collection of navigational paraphernalia, model ships and paintings. Photos also give a glimpse into Leith's old quayside, prior to its decommissioning and subsequent regeneration.

The Shore

MAP PAGE 108

The best way to absorb Leith's history and seafaring connections is to take a stroll along **The Shore**, a tenement-lined road running alongside the Water of Leith. Until the mid-nineteenth century, this was a bustling and cosmopolitan **harbour**, visited by ships from all over the world, but as vessels became increasingly large, they moored up at custom-built docks built beyond the original quays; these days, only a handful of boats are permanently moored here. Instead, the focus is on the cluster of **pubs and restaurants** lining the street, many of which spill tables and chairs out onto the cobbled pavement on sunny days. And the culinary landscape is good; Leith has two Michelin-starred restaurants – *The Kitchin* and *Martin Wishart* – within a few hundred yards of each other.

The historic buildings along this stretch include the imposing Neoclassical **Custom House**, used for occasional public exhibitions and private events; the round **signal tower**, which was originally constructed as a windmill; and the turrets and towers of the **Sailors' Home**, built in Scots Baronial style in the 1880s as a dosshouse for seafarers.

Royal Yacht Britannia

MAP PAGE 108

Ocean Terminal. www.royalyachtbritannia. co.uk. Charge.

Moored alongside **Ocean Terminal**, a huge Terence Conran-designed shopping and entertainment centre, the **Royal Yacht Britannia** is one of the world's most famous ships. Launched in 1953 at John Brown's shipyard on Clydeside, *Britannia* was used by the royal family for 44 years for state visits, diplomatic functions and royal holidays. Leith acquired the vessel following decommission in 1997, against the wishes of many of the Royal Family, who felt that scuttling would have been a more dignified end. Alongside *Britannia*, the sleek former royal sailing yacht, *Bloodhound*, is also on view (Sept–June).

Visits to *Britannia* begin in the **visitor centre**, on the second floor of Ocean Terminal, where royal

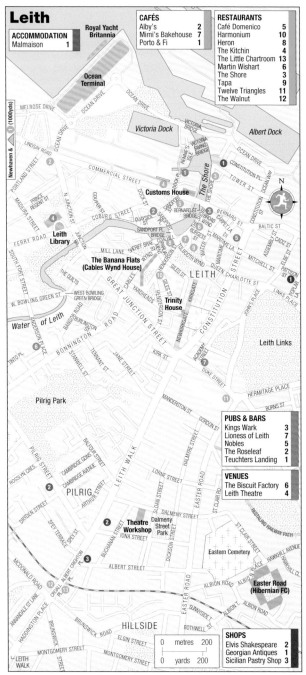

Leith

ACCOMMODATION

Malmaison	1

CAFÉS

Alby's	2
Mimi's Bakehouse	7
Porto & Fi	1

RESTAURANTS

Café Domenico	5
Harmonium	10
Heron	8
The Kitchin	4
The Little Chartroom	13
Martin Wishart	6
The Shore	3
Tapa	9
Twelve Triangles	11
The Walnut	12

PUBS & BARS

Kings Wark	3
Lioness of Leith	7
Nobles	5
The Roseleaf	2
Teuchters Landing	1

VENUES

The Biscuit Factory	6
Leith Theatre	4

SHOPS

Elvis Shakespeare	2
Georgian Antiques	1
Sicilian Pastry Shop	3

The Siege of Leith

In 1560, three thousand French troops found themselves caught up in a pivotal point in Scotland's history as the **Reformation** fuelled religious and political turmoil. The French had originally been asked to help protect Mary of Guise, Regent of Scotland, from the English in 1548, but Protestant Scots gradually turned against their protectors, coming to regard them more as occupiers than saviours. Battles between the two sides began in 1559, with the heavily outnumbered but disciplined French soon gaining the upper hand. The Scots issued a request to England for help and for the first time in history the Scots would fight side by side with "**the Auld Enemy**". Therein followed a period of unimaginable suffering as the French were ordered to defend their base in Leith "to the last of their blood and breath". Holed up within the town walls and with an English blockade of the port and cannonballs flying overhead, the French troops and Leith's townsfolk began to starve, reduced to eating cats, dogs and rats, according to contemporary accounts. The stalemate finally ended with Mary of Guise's death in June 1560, and the signing of the **Treaty of Edinburgh** the following month, effectively ending the centuries-old **Auld Alliance** between Scotland and France.

holiday snaps and video clips of the ship's most famous moments, which included the 1983 evacuation of Aden and the British handover of Hong Kong in 1997, are shown. An audio handset is then handed out and you're allowed to roam around the yacht: the **bridge**, the **engine room**, the **officers' mess** and a large part of the **state apartments**. The ship has been kept largely as it was when in service, with a well-preserved 1950s dowdiness that the audio-guide loyally attributes to Queen Elizabeth II's good taste and astute frugality in the lean post-War years. Certainly, the atmosphere is a far cry from the opulent splendour that many expect. You can stay on the former floating palace, which has been reimagined as luxury hotel *Fingal*, which has a two AA-Rosette restaurant, stargazing decks and traditionally styled cabins.

Newhaven
MAP PAGE 108

The old village (now suburb) of **Newhaven** was established by James IV at the start of the sixteenth century as an alternative shipbuilding centre to Leith: his massive warship, the *Great Michael* was built here. Newhaven has also been a ferry station and an important fishing centre, landing some six million oysters a year at the height of its success in the 1860s. Today, the chief pleasure is a stroll around the stone **harbour**, which still has a pleasantly salty feel, with a handful of boats tied up alongside or resting gently on the tidal mud.

Newhaven harbour

Shops

Elvis Shakespeare

MAP PAGE 108

347 Leith Walk. www.elvis
shakespeare.com.

Leith's favourite record and book
shop, specializing in secondhand
literature and rare vinyl with a
subtle bias towards punk, post
punk and indie. The shop also
hosts regular live-music sessions
courtesy of local artists.

Georgian Antiques

MAP PAGE 108

10 Pattison St. www.georgianantiques.net.

Enormous multi-tiered warehouse
bulging with antiquities small
and large. There's something for
everyone here, with items ranging
from fine furniture and taxidermy
to old golf clubs and riding boots.

Sicilian Pastry Shop

MAP PAGE 108

14–16 Albert St. www.thesicilianpastry
shoplimited.co.uk.

A brilliant little family shop selling
sweet and colourful cakes, mostly
Sicilian in style – featuring lots of

Malteser slices at Mimi's Bakehouse

cream. Not really a café but it does
sell a punchy espresso here, too.

Cafés

Alby's

MAP PAGE 108

8 Portland Place. www.albysleith.co.uk.

Forget a soggy cheese sanger, *Alby's*
is all about doorstop-sized focaccia
sarnies overflowing with tasty
fillings, from battered chicken with
sweet and sour sauce, sesame and
chiu chow mayo, ginger spring
onion, pickled chilli and shredded
napa cabbage, to pan-fried mackerel
with dill-spiked aioli, slow-roasted
vine tomatoes, smoked chilli,
matchstick chips and rocket. The
sides are just as creative: fried corn
ribs and chimichurri, Korean-style
fried celeriac, and the like. £

Mimi's Bakehouse

MAP PAGE 108

63 Shore. www.mimisbakehouse.com.

Family-run, vintage-styled teashop;
its lovingly crafted cakes, tray
bakes and scones make for an
appetizingly colourful counter
display. The light lunches on offer
are a treat too, but best of all is the
tiered afternoon tea platter. £

Porto & Fi

MAP PAGE 108

47 Main St, Newhaven. www.portofi.com.

A bright and breezy café that morphs
into a laidback restaurant, not far
from Newhaven's old stone harbour.
Wash down tempting cakes with
freshly brewed coffee in the day
or, after dark, pick from a seafood-
leaning menu that includes smoked
haddock and cullen skink risotto. £££

Restaurants

Café Domenico

MAP PAGE 108

30 Sandport St. www.cafedomenico.co.uk.

A good-value authentic backstreet
Italian restaurant (not a café)

that dishes up damn fine Italian fast food and takeaway toasted sandwiches. £££

Harmonium

MAP PAGE 108
60 Henderson St. www.harmoniumbar.co.uk.

From the team behind Glasgow's famous music record shop/vegan café *Mono*, *Harmonium* is pushing the boundaries of vegan cuisine with its cutting-edge gastrobar grub. Oysters, crab, caviar, quarter pounders and even black pudding feature on its menu – in interpretive plant form at least – and lunchtime specials are a snip. £££

Heron

MAP PAGE 108
87–91A Henderson St. www.heron.scot.

A bright and breezy restaurant – all whitewashed walls and pale woods – by Tomás Gormley and Sam Yorke, the hottest names on Edinburgh's culinary scene. The menu draws on the natural larder of Scotland, transforming simple, seasonal ingredients into playful, perfectly executed dishes. Standouts include the Orkney scallop with ponzu and quail spiked with cherry and chard. The Michelin team agrees – slapping a much-coveted star on the restaurant within a year of its opening. Opt for the lunchtime set menu if you're on a budget. ££££

The Kitchin

MAP PAGE 108
78 Commercial Quay. www.thekitchin.com.

Opened in 2006 by celebrity chef Tom Kitchin and the winner – less than six months later – of a Michelin star, the motto here is "from nature to plate" – a philosophy that ensures the freshest ingredients. Try the "Celebration of the Season" menu, where you might find braised Highland Wagyu with a bone-marrow sauce or boned and rolled pig's head. Vegetarian options are available. Opt for the three-course set lunch

The Shore

menus if you're on a budget or splash out on the Chef's Surprise Tasting menu for five courses of pure indulgence. ££££

The Little Chartroom

MAP PAGE 108
30–31 Albert Place. www.thelittle chartroom.com.

This dinky destination, just a short amble from the city centre, offers seasonally focussed set menus featuring such combinations as smoked pigeon, celeriac, plum and walnut and desserts like rhubarb, white chocolate and pistachio éclair – and it's scooped a Michelin listing, no less. ££££

Martin Wishart

MAP PAGE 108
52 Shore. www.restaurantmartinwishart.co.uk.

The eponymous chef is one of the trailblazers on the Scottish culinary scene – and the first Michelin-star holder in Edinburgh. Expect highly accomplished and exquisitely presented French-inspired dishes featuring Scottish-sourced fish and meat. A three-course lunch (Wed–Fri) is the best value at £52.50, while a six-course evening tasting menu will set you back £125. ££££

The Shore

MAP PAGE 108

3–4 Shore. www.fishersrestaurants.co.uk.
Well-lived-in bar-restaurant with huge mirrors, wood panelling and aproned waiters who serve up good sea (and land) food at reasonable prices. Live jazz, folk and general hubbub float through from the adjoining bar where you'll find a wide selection of snacks on offer, including trout and herb croquettes. £££

Tapa

MAP PAGE 108

19 Shore Place. www.tapaedinburgh.co.uk.
Authentic Spanish restaurant in an attractive old warehouse, offering good-value tapas and a superb sherry list. The lunch deal is a bargain and includes the standout tapa, aubergine crisps with honey. ££

Twelve Triangles

MAP PAGE 108

148 Duke St. www.twelvetriangles.co.uk.
Unmissable brunch joint and bakery that makes just about everything, right down to the pickles and condiments, from scratch. The

The Kitchin

offerings change regularly; you might carve into a plate of ham and eggs with sourdough, sauerkraut and beetroot apple relish or dip your crust into a rich shakshuka. ££

The Walnut

MAP PAGE 108

9 Croall Place, Leith Walk.
www.thewalnutedinburgh.co.uk.
One of Leith Walk's most popular neighbourhood diners thanks to its affordable, solid home-style British cooking and its bring-your-own bottle policy. Dishes might include beef shin and haggis croquette followed by curried cauliflower and potato pie; save room for the strawberry custard tart with elderflower ice cream. £££

Pubs and Bars

Kings Wark

MAP PAGE 108

36 Shore. www.thekingswarkpub.com.
Restored fifteenth-century harbourside pub with attached restaurant. Its picturesque interior of stone walls and corniced ceilings gives an ambience that's changed very little since the days of the old sea dogs telling tales at the bar.

Lioness of Leith

MAP PAGE 108

21–25 Duke St. www.thelionessofleith.co.uk.
With pop art on the walls, an arcade machine in the corner and a table made out of a pinball machine, this Victorian boozer certainly looks young for its age. There's regular live music at weekends, a good kitchen and a loyal local following.

Nobles

MAP PAGE 108

44a Constitution St. www.noblesbarleith.
co.uk.
Handsome Victorian bar with more than its fair share of stained glass, chandeliers and wood panelling, this is a good place to sup a posh

Teuchters Landing

cocktail or two. The bar's kitchen operates in gastropub territory with a particularly fine dessert to look out for: apple mousse, toasted meringue and honey oat biscuit with spiced rum and blackberry syrup.

The Roseleaf

MAP PAGE 108
23–24 Sandport Place. www.roseleaf.co.uk.
Chintzy-cool local that's a little off the beaten track but worth the trip for the pot-tails alone – funky cocktails like the "Breakfast Club" (Finnish vodka with elderflower, mint and citrus fruits) served in vintage teapots.

Teuchters Landing

MAP PAGE 108
1 Dock Place. www.teuchtersbar.co.uk.
Spilling out onto a bespoke pontoon, with seductive harbour views, *Teuchters'* beer garden is the ideal place to while away a braw, bricht summer's afternoon. The pub itself, converted from a waiting room for the decommissioned Leith to Aberdeen steamboat, is a delightful, traditional-style free house dissected into a genial collection of nooks and snugs, with an overcrowded

bar and a superfluously large whisky selection.

Venues

The Biscuit Factory

MAP PAGE 108
4–6 Anderson Place. www.biscuitfactory.
co.uk.
Arts and fashion venue in an old industrial estate warehouse. Besides the workshops and gin distillery, the building hosts an eclectic range of events, including after-hours warehouse parties; food and craft markets; beer and music festivals; and interesting pop-up restaurants.

Leith Theatre

MAP PAGE 108
28–30 Ferry Rd. www.leiththeatre.co.uk.
Having undergone a staggered refurbishment after three decades of abandonment, this delightful Art Deco auditorium has reopened its doors again to host major city events like the Hidden Door Festival (see page 87) and August Festival Fringe shows. Generally, the focus is on music recitals and old film screenings, with the occasional nod to local culture and history.

West Edinburgh

Suburban west Edinburgh has its own fair share of touristic temptations, chiefly that of the enormous zoo that covers a good tranche of Corstorphine Hill's southern slopes and Murrayfield Stadium, home of the Scottish rugby team. There's also much history to be discovered here among the ancient satellite villages, since subsumed by the city's exponential growth in the past century. The old Roman settlement of Cramond has a familiar seaside town feel to it, while just inland, Lauriston Castle is one of only a handful still standing within the city's boundaries. Chimneys still punch up above the skyline, frequently delivering west Edinburgh's characteristic malty aroma; a reminder of the city's brewing heritage originally powered by the coal delivered along the Union Canal and the railways that crisscross the landscape.

Edinburgh Zoo

MAP PAGE 115
134 Corstorphine Rd. www.edinburghzoo.
org.uk. Charge. Buses #12, #26 & #31
westbound from Princes Street.

Draped across an eighty-acre site on the slopes of Corstorphine Hill, **Edinburgh Zoo** has transformed itself in recent years into a modern conservation and recreation park success and one of the city's must-see attractions. Appealingly set in the midst of a botanic garden, the enclosures offer plenty of opportunities for up-close animal encounters. The heralded arrival of giant pandas in 2011 bolstered the zoo's already impressive collection (though Tian Tian and Yang Guang are set to return to China in 2023), augmented more recently by the birth of baby red panda Ruby to parents Ginger and Bruce in 2021; and two years later, an infant L'Hoest's monkey joined brother Butembo and parents Sheli and Jamal. It's a bit of an uphill hike to the far end of the zoo but once there you can admire the city views, then wander back down passing under the reinforced-glass tiger tunnel, past the Asiatic lions and sun bears, and arrive at the enormous dedicated chimpanzee research centre. Unless it's raining, the place is permanently packed with kids, and the zoo's most famous attraction for youngsters is its **penguin parade**, when rangers entice a waddle of the flightless birds to leave their enclosure for a short circuit lined with admiring spectators.

Red panda at the zoo

Murrayfield Stadium

MAP PAGE 115
West Stand, Roseburn St. www.scottish
rugby.org/murrayfield-stadium/tours.
Charge.

The home of Scottish rugby since
1925 when, on its **Murrayfield**
debut, the home side scraped a
narrow win over England in front
of 70,000 spectators. Although
similar successes are rather thin
on the ground these days, today's
modern panorama-hogging
stadium – the largest in Scotland
– must still be an intimidating
prospect for the biannual visitors
from south of the border. To
witness the place from the players'
point of view, join one of the
regular tours that focuses on the
inner workings of the stadium,
with a 90min anecdote-laden
exposure to the commentary
box, dressing room and trophy
cabinets. The highlight of the
visit is unquestionably the trot

Six Nations rugby match at Murrayfield

out onto the pitch through the
tunnel to the imagined roar of a
capacity crowd.

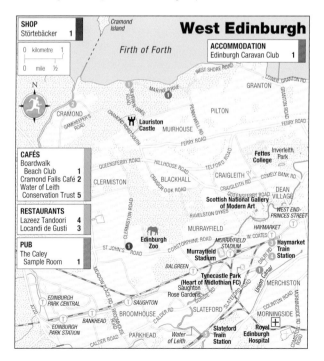

Lauriston Castle

Lauriston Castle

MAP PAGE 115

2a Cramond Rd South. www.edinburgh
museums.org.uk. Charge for house,
gardens free. Bus no.41 westbound from
Princes Street.

A short walk from the popular
seaside settlement of Cramond, this
sixteenth-century tower house with
Jacobean-style extensions still looks
the part in its rural parkland setting.
Its north face gazes out across the
croquet lawn to the choppy Firth of
Forth, while the delightful adjacent
Japanese walled garden offers respite
from a bitter northerly.

Approached from its southern
flank across a large meadow, the
building itself is most interesting
for its interior. Bequeathed in
1926 to Edinburgh Council under
the strict proviso that it remained
unchanged, **Lauriston Castle**
gives a rare and charming insight
into a lived-in Edwardian-Scottish
country pile.

Cramond

MAP PAGE 115

5 miles northwest of the town centre.
Bus #41 westbound from central Princes
Street. For tide times, either check the

noticeboard on shore or text 'CRAMOND'
to 81400.

The enduring image of **Cramond** is
of step-gabled whitewashed houses
tumbling down the hillside to the
waterfront, though it also has the
foundations of a Roman fort, and
a tower house, church, inn and
mansion, all from the seventeenth
century. The best reason to come
here is to enjoy a stroll around and
a bit of fresh air. The **walk** along
the wide promenade that traces
the shoreline offers great views of
the Forth; or head out across the
causeway to the uninhabited bird
sanctuary of Cramond Island –
though beware that the causeway
disappears as high tide approaches
and can leave you stranded if you
get your timings wrong. Aim to get
to and from the island within the
two hours either side of low tide.

Inland of Cramond, there's another
pleasant walk along a tree-lined path
by the River Almond, past former
mills and their adjoining cottages
towards the sixteenth-century Old
Cramond Bridge. From here, you
can either continue upstream or cross
the bridge and head back towards
the coast within the grounds of

Canal boat trips

Surely the best way to experience the Union Canal is to take to the water by way of a boat trip; there are a few companies along the stretch that offer excursions and even boat hire.

If you have the means and time available, head out of town to Linlithgow, where the fascinating trips on offer include a crossing of the Avon aqueduct, the longest and tallest in Scotland, or stick to Edinburgh to watch the city slip by over a leisurely cream tea.

LINLITHGOW CANAL CENTRE

Manse Road Basin. www.lucs.org.uk. Town cruises: July to mid-Aug daily & April–Sept weekends depart every half-hour 1.30–4pm; 25min. £5. Aqueduct cruises: April–Sept Sat & Sun 2pm; 2hr 30min. £12. Falkirk Wheel cruises: Around 4 per year, check website for dates; 5hr 30min. £30.

RE-UNION CANAL BOATS

Fountainbridge. www.re-union.org.uk. Afternoon tea cruise (occasional) Sun 2pm; 2hr. £28.

Dalmeny Estate, laced by wonderful little-known beaches and forest walks. There is also a stately home – Dalmeny House (see page 131) – and the evocative baronial-style Barnbougle Castle poised alone on the water's edge.

Union Canal

MAP PAGE 115

Begins at Fountainbridge, a short walk west of the centre.

Like an environmental lance, the **Union Canal** pierces deep into the heart of formerly industrialized west-central Edinburgh, bringing with it a perfect bike-friendly opportunity to escape the confines of the city away from traffic. Passing wildfowl, barges and lofty viaducts, the route swiftly shifts through the city's suburbs before breaking out into delightful tree enclosed countryside en route to Falkirk, home of the Kelpies – 30m-tall metallic horsehead sculptures – and the Falkirk Wheel, a unique engineering feat that lifts barges between the Union, Forth and Clyde canals.

Originally built in 1822, the canal was an important artery for the industrial revolution, delivering coal to power Falkirk's iron-casting works and Edinburgh's many breweries as well as to heat the swelling number of residential houses in the capital. Just two decades after its opening, the construction of railways in the area dealt a hammer blow to its prosperity. The canal went into a near-terminal spiral of decline, stopped in its tracks in recent years by a reflective political will to protect Scotland's heritage and fragile ecosystems.

A barge on the Union Canal

Edinburgh for kids

Look at a map of town and it's pleasingly evident that Edinburgh's green belt makes up more than half the city's acreage. With its landscape of hills, forests and river stitched together by canal and coastal paths and crisscrossed by dedicated cycleways, Edinburgh is the ideal place for children to experience the great outdoors with the benefits of an urban environment close at hand. When the weather's against you, there's a large number of child-friendly attractions in which to seek refuge, many of which are free.

Top 5 things to do on a rainy day

MUSEUM OF SCOTLAND
(See page 59)
Cavernous and interactive, the Museum of Scotland is a perfect spot for kids to play games, dig for fossils and program robots, while for little tots there's a colourful sensory room befit with musical stepping stones, a Wendy house, and shadow puppets.

DYNAMIC EARTH
(See page 69)
Subterranean, family-friendly exploration into the geology of our planet, with numerous interactive exhibits, an earthquake simulation and a 4D cinema finale.

CAMERA OBSCURA & WORLD OF ILLUSIONS
(See page 40)
A city favourite for kids of all ages, with floor after floor of holograms, optical illusions, mirrors and hands-on exhibits.

EICA CLIP AND CLIMB
(See page 129)

At the enormous climbing centre just west of Edinburgh, Clip and Climb is a series of challenges designed for children (4 years and over) that includes climbing walls, huge spheres and tubes to scale as well as jumps and slides.

EDINBURGH DUNGEON
(See page 76)

One for older kids, Edinburgh Dungeon seeks to simultaneously scare and entertain with spine-chilling rides and talking severed heads that take you on a journey into Edinburgh's gruesome medieval past.

Top 5 fair-weather things to do with kids

EDINBURGH ZOO
(See page 114)

Pandas, parks and penguin parades; Edinburgh Zoo is the number-one child-friendly destination in town.

JUPITER ARTLAND
(See page 114)

To the eyes of a parent, it's a dramatic sculpture park in the West Lothian countryside, but to kids, Jupiter Artland is simply an extensive adventure playground. There are sculptures and trees to climb, water features to play in and endless opportunities to run around and explore in a safe environment.

MIDLOTHIAN SNOWSPORTS CENTRE
(See page 115)

Just outside the city boundary on the northernmost slopes of the Pentland hills, your kids will love jumping into a tyre and hurling themselves down the slippery slopes at dizzying speeds. As well as tubing, there's a decently precipitous dry slope for all year skiing and boarding.

THE YARD
(See page 101)

Brilliant organic adventure playground made out of reclaimed junk; designed by the team behind BBC's *DIY SOS* programme for carefree play.

PORTOBELLO BEACH
(See page 71)

Good old-fashioned British beach resort with golden sands, play parks, a promenade and fish and chips.

Shop

Störtebäcker

MAP PAGE 115

38 St John's Rd. www.stortebacker.co.uk.
Surely the world's smallest
bakery, housed in the "wee shop"
with standing room for just two
people. Luckily, there's plentiful
counter space for a veritable
bounty of outstanding home-
made (literally) sourdoughs,
cakes, pastries and tarts. Loosely
translated as "harassed baker",
this enterprise is the brainchild
of two German friends with a
passion for the *Torten* and *Brot*
of home.

Cafés

Boardwalk Beach Club

MAP PAGE 115

50 Marine Drive, Silverknowes.
www.facebook.com/boardwalkbeachclub.
Unique standalone café with
unhindered sea views and a
clientele that ebbs and flows
depending on the weather; chairs
spill out beyond the patio to the

lawn for those rare balmy summer
days. There's nothing surprising
on the menu – panini, soup, cake
et al – but it's the quality of the
food and drink that would make
this place stand out from the
competition, if there was any. ££

Cramond Falls Café

MAP PAGE 115

10 School Brae. www.facebook.com/
CramondFallsCafe.
Taking its name from the delightful
adjacent waterfall, this café,
converted from a seventeenth-
century mill, makes for an idyllic
distraction on a saunter up
Cramond's River Almond. You can
have a hearty cooked breakfast here
or a freshly baked scone – if you
time it right. Plus, there are plenty
of health-conscious and veggie
options, too. ££

Water of Leith Conservation Trust

MAP PAGE 115

24 Lanark Rd. www.waterofleith.org.uk.
An almost compulsory stop
if you're walking the Water of
Leith. Dunk a couple of biscuits
in a pleasingly cheap cuppa then

Boardwalk Beach Club

The Caley Sample Room

have a quick browse around the small, free exhibition on the river's wildlife and industrial heritage, which includes a child-friendly "interactive zone". £

Restaurants

Lazeez Tandoori

MAP PAGE 115
191 Dalry Rd. www.lazeeztandoori.co.uk.
Cunningly disguised as an insalubrious kebab joint, *Lazeez* defies all presuppositions with its sensational Punjabi home-style cooking; among the best in town and with plenty of heat. The home-made *kheer* (Indian rice pudding) – the result of twelve hours of cooking – is light, delicious and necessarily cleansing. £

Locanda de Gusti

MAP PAGE 115
102 Dalry Rd. www.locandadegusti.com.
Brought up in a large Neapolitan family, owner Rosario Sartore knows his cipollas when it comes to true Italian home cooking. Kitted out like a modern-day osteria, the colourful decor is

outshone by the vibrancy of the food. Grilled seafood is usually the star of the show here, though the home-made pasta dishes are just as tempting – garlicky *paccheri* tossed with lobster, crab, piennolo tomatoes and a splash of brandy or the orecchiette with slow-cooked lamb shoulder, tomato passata and basil. £££

Pub

The Caley Sample Room

MAP PAGE 115
42–58 Angle Park Terrace.
www.caleysampleroom.co.uk.
Named after, although not affiliated to, Edinburgh's oldest surviving brewery, The Caledonian (sited in the delightful Victorian factory nearby), this pub-restaurant proudly reserves a tap for its namesake's famous Deuchar's IPA. If that's not for your palate, then there's a feast of guest taps that changes daily and bottled ales to cheer the dourest CAMRA inspector. The pub also has a good rep for home-made gastropub grub.

South Edinburgh

Stubbornly middle class, leafy and Labour-voting, the political constituency of Edinburgh South encompasses some of the city's most desirable and cosmopolitan postcodes, including Newington, Marchmont, Bruntsfield and Morningside. Fringed and softened by the green expanse of the Meadows, Newington and Marchmont have long been home to a vibrant, multinational mix of well-off students and young families, while Bruntsfield, with its vintage furniture shops and Farrow & Ball-painted brunch spots, stakes its claim as the Hampstead of the North. House prices spike even further as Bruntsfield morphs into the mansions of archetypally genteel Morningside. There aren't many sights as such, though you can easily lose yourself amid the trails of Blackford Hill Nature Reserve and – at least in winter – go stargazing in the Royal Observatory. The real pleasure here is simply wandering at will, following your nose to artisan coffee shops, pungent cheese shops, sweet-scented bakeries and bistros.

Newington

MAP PAGE 124

Blending into the city's grittier Southside in the lee of Salisbury

Edinburgh University halls, Newington

Crags at one end, and stretching out to the handsome Victorian townhouses of the Grange at the other, **Newington** is predominantly young, buzzing and ever-changing. Home to the bulk of Edinburgh University and its huge and multi-ethnic academic population, the area has seen swanky student accommodation blocks mushroom in recent years, with an ever-growing crop of shops, bars, cafés and restaurants. Newington is likewise the epicentre of the **Fringe** come August, home to both the Pleasance Courtyard and Assembly Roxy, and with the Gilded Balloon, Pleasance Dome and Underbelly all setting up temporary shop and swelling the youthful population even further. Arts venue Summerhall (see page 127), meanwhile, is both a festival uber-hub and a year-round hipster fixture, the most exciting addition to Edinburgh's cultural scene in years.

Cherry blossom in The Meadows

The Meadows

MAP PAGE 124

An elm-lined, fan-shaped park tracing the boundaries of Newington, Marchmont and Tollcross, **The Meadows** – like Princes Street Gardens – began life as a loch, in this case supplying much of Edinburgh's drinking water. At the instigation of Sir Thomas Hope, it was drained in the eighteenth century and a law passed in 1827 forbade construction on the site. The classic **urban park** that emerged is a joy: crisscrossed by cycle and pedestrian paths and bordered by food trucks, kiosks and cafés, it comes into its own in spring and summer when people flock here from nearby tenements for impromptu barbecues, games of cricket and al-fresco prosecco. With the background thrum of djembe drums, the waft of sizzling veggie burgers and a babylon of voices, it has a much more bohemian vibe than Princes Street Gardens, and is often akin to a low-key music festival. Unsurprisingly, it's often at its busiest in August, with various tented venues springing up and festivalgoers basking in the sun.

Bruntsfield and Morningside

MAP PAGE 124
Bus #5, #11, #15, #16, #23 or #36.
Unfurling to the southwest of the Meadows, **Bruntsfield Links** is the only remnant of the old Burgh Muir, an ancient five-square-mile expanse of grazing land with a chequered history, including use as a hanging ground and quarantine area for plague victims. To the west of the Links is **Bruntsfield** itself, a wealthy enclave populated by independent shops, cafés and restaurants, and no stranger to the big screen, appearing in both *The Prime of Miss Jean Brodie* and, more recently, *Trainspotting T2*. Past the final curve of Bruntsfield Place, the ancient thoroughfare of Morningside Road climbs dead south into one of Edinburgh's (and Scotland's) wealthiest, most satirized and – according to a 2022 survey – happiest suburbs. Famous as the fictional home of the aforementioned Miss Jean Brodie, Morningside only occasionally lives up to the clichés. While the surrounding streets are home to all manner of eye-poppingly expensive

Morningside

and antique-filled charity shops, plus the iconic and infamously intimidating *Canny Man's* pub (see page 127). Don't miss the late Art Deco splendour of the Dominion Cinema on Newbattle Terrace, by far the most luxurious place in Edinburgh to catch a film; the velvet-lined lobbies are filled with pre-selfie photographic portraits of visiting stars.

The Hermitage of Braid and Blackford Hill Local Nature Reserve

MAP PAGE 124
Braid Road. www.edinburgh.gov.uk. Bus #11 or #15.

Way off the tourist trail and probably all the better for it, this wonderful, ancient woodland-designated **nature reserve** is accessible from Braid Road on the southern fringes of Morningside. The near 150-acre site is at its most dramatic around the steep gorge

Victorian confections, Morningside Road itself is lined with tenements and has a surprisingly down-to-earth feel; a friendly, bustling mix of bistros, artisan food outlets

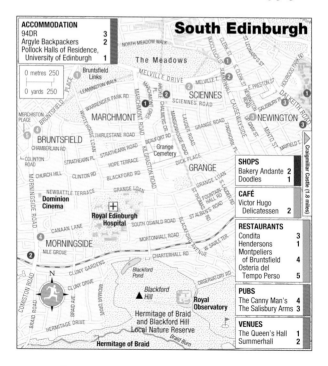

South Edinburgh

ACCOMMODATION
94DR — 3
Argyle Backpackers — 2
Pollock Halls of Residence, University of Edinburgh — 1

SHOPS
Bakery Andante — 2
Doodles — 1

CAFÉ
Victor Hugo Delicatessen — 2

RESTAURANTS
Condita — 3
Hendersons — 1
Montpeliers of Bruntsfield — 4
Osteria del Tempo Perso — 5

PUBS
The Canny Man's — 4
The Salisbury Arms — 3

VENUES
The Queen's Hall — 1
Summerhall — 2

that slices through the **Hermitage of Braid**, with paths threading across precipitous slopes covered in mature elm, ash, beech, sycamore, rowan and oak, themselves some of the city's tallest trees. **Hermitage House** nestles in glorious seclusion in the middle of the glen, accessed by a tarmac drive. Built in 1785 by local architect Robert Burn, its castellated Gothic Revival stylings would be echoed in turn by Burn's son, William, one of the pioneers of the Scots Baronial style. Today, the hermitage is category A-listed and home to a **Visitor Centre**, where you can pick up maps for the reserve's orienteering course. Nearby is a formerly derelict **walled garden** and extravagant **doocot** (dovecot), originally built to supply a long-gone fortified castle. Once containing almost 2000 sandstone nest boxes, the doocot presumably satisfied what must have been one almighty appetite for pigeon pie. Myriad volunteer groups, meanwhile, have transformed the walled land into a **community wildlife garden** in recent years, a work in progress geared towards wildflowers and native medicinal plants. To the west, paths lead to the wide-open spaces of **Blackford Hill**, with magnificent views north over the cityscape and south to the Pentland and Moorfoot Hills.

Royal Observatory

MAP PAGE 124
Blackford Hill. www.roe.ac.uk. Charge. Bus #24 or #41.

While Scotland is now at the forefront of space science and satellite technology, Edinburgh's **Royal Observatory** has been scanning the heavens from its prime position on Blackford Hill since 1896. Recognized worldwide for its contributions to, and development of, astronomy, the observatory is also one of the architectural landmarks of south Edinburgh, its distinctive form bookended by octagonal towers

supporting copper-sheathed, cylindrical telescope housing.

Astronomy Evenings take in the original **Victorian telescope dome** and in winter, weather depending, you'll witness the firmament like you've never seen it before. Note that tours are held on a strictly prebooked basis and demand is higher in winter when it's best to book well in advance.

Craigmillar Castle

MAP PAGE 124
Craigmillar Castle Road. www.historic environment.scot. Charge; HES. Bus #8, #33 or #49.

Craigmillar Castle sits amid a small tranche of green belt some five miles south of the city centre, offering an atmospheric, untrammelled contrast to packed Edinburgh Castle. The oldest part of the complex is the **L-shaped tower house**, which dates back to the early 1400s – this remains substantially intact, and the **great hall**, with its resplendent late Gothic chimneypiece, is in good enough shape to be rented out for functions. Once occasionally used by Mary, Queen of Scots, the **tower house**, however, was abandoned to its picturesque decay in the mid-eighteenth century.

Royal Observatory

Montpeliers of Bruntsfield

Shops

Bakery Andante

MAP PAGE 124

352 Morningside Rd. www.bakeryandante.
co.uk. Bus #5, #11, #15, #16, #23 or #36.
Award-winning artisan bakery selling
a range of delicious sourdough breads,
none more so than its unsurpassably
crusty Covenanter. The almond
croissants are just as heavenly. This
kind of quality doesn't come cheap
but look out for morning bargains
in the shape of half-price, still-fresh
loaves unsold from the previous day.

Doodles

MAP PAGE 124

29 Marchmont Crescent. www.doodles
scotland.co.uk. Bus #5, #24 or #41.
Edinburgh's original and best paint-
your-own pottery workshop. If you
have kids in tow and you're going
to be in town for more than four
days (the time it takes to glaze and
fire your masterpiece), this is a great
rainy-day diversion.

Café

Victor Hugo Delicatessen

MAP PAGE 124

26–27 Melville Terrace, Marchmont.
www.victorhugodeli.com.

Even on the darkest and coldest of
winter days, locals huddle around
the gingham-clad outdoor tables
of this Meadows-Marchmont
landmark. In business since the
50s, the place has recently been
refurbished, though the famous
black-and-scarlet exterior, and deli
classics – think eggs Benedict and
pastrami on rye – remain. ££

Restaurants

Condita

MAP PAGE 124

15 Salisbury Pl, Newington. www.condita.
co.uk.

This intimate, six-table Michelin-
starred restaurant is shrouded in
mystery: the only information
revealed on its website is that it
offers a surprise tasting menu (£140/
person) by chef Conor Toomey. If
you're a fussy eater, stay away: there is
only one menu, no tweaks to dishes
for personal preferences, and no
changes on the night. However, if
you're happy to trust in the culinary
expertise of the team, you're in for
a treat. Dishes are experimental yet
confident; think poached mussel
topped with a seaweed emulsion
and caviar, cradled in a potato and
squid-ink edible shell. A pescatarian
and vegetarian menu are available if
prebooked. Reservation only. ££££

Hendersons

MAP PAGE 124

7–13 Barclay Place. www.hendersons
restaurant.com.

Much-loved foodie institution
Hendersons is back – with a different
location and a new owner. The
Hanover Street original may
have shuttered in 2020 following
the pandemic, but owner Janet
Henderson's grandson, Barrie, revived
the restaurant near Bruntsfield Links
a year later. The focus is on vegetarian
and vegan food – the popular plant-
based haggis is a mainstay, joining
new dishes like cauliflower steak and
beetroot burger. £££

Montpeliers of Bruntsfield

MAP PAGE 124

159–161 Bruntsfield Place.
www.montpeliersedinburgh.co.uk. Bus
#11, #15, #16, #23 or #36.

The well-manicured pillar of
Bruntsfield's dining establishment,
and a rare constant in Edinburgh's
formidable turnover of bars and
restaurants. You'll likely need to
book if you want to enjoy one of its
famous trad brunches or well-regarded
mains; try the confit duck leg with
caramelized apple and peppercorn
sauce. ££

Osteria del Tempo Perso

MAP PAGE 124

208 Bruntsfield Place. www.mytempo
perso.com. Bus #11, #15, #16, #23 or #36.

The Bruntsfield *bambino* of a
Lazio-based papa, this award-
winning, family-run affair is a
more authentic Italian experience
than many. A dazzling mosaic-tiled
ceiling, inimitably informal service,
ravishingly garlicky pasta and a
better-than-moussaka *parmigiana
alla melanzane* are all testament to
the proverbial *dolce vita*. £££

Pubs

The Canny Man's

MAP PAGE 124

239 Morningside Rd. www.cannymans.
co.uk. Bus #5, #11, #15, #16, #23 or #36.

More Churchillian time capsule
than pub, and an exquisite – if
often frostily exclusive – antidote
to Edinburgh's interior-design
arms race; even the dust used to
be antique. "The best pub in the
world" according to Rick Stein, and
he might not be far off. Just don't
necessarily expect a warm welcome.

The Salisbury Arms

MAP PAGE 124

58 Dalkeith Rd, Newington. www.the
salisburyarmsedinburgh.co.uk.

A gorgeous Victorian townhouse set
comfortably back from busy Dalkeith
Road, this countrified gastropub is
perfect for a post-Arthur's Seat pint.
The leafy, partially secluded beer
garden is one of Edinburgh's hidden
delights, while a roaring fire, decent
mains and pleasant staff make for an
inviting interior. £££

Venues

The Queen's Hall

MAP PAGE 124

85–89 Clerk Street, Newington.
www.thequeenshall.net.

There's nothing quite like
an intimate jazz or classical
performance in this hushed former
church, one of Edinburgh's best-
loved live-music venues. Also stages
folk and world music, plus the odd
pop or rock gig. Comes into its
own during the Fringe.

Summerhall

MAP PAGE 124

Summerhall Square, Newington.
www.summerhall.co.uk.

Edinburgh's largest, most ambitious
multidiscipline arts, artisan and
tech hub – everything from
cutting-edge theatre to craft
brewing; live music to club nights.
The onsite *Royal Dick* bar reflects
Summerhall's previous incarnation
as a veterinary school, replete with
specimen cases, microscopes and an
on-site gin distillery.

Summerhall

Day-trips

Cast your line just beyond Edinburgh's tight margins and you'll bear witness to tantalizing glimpses of what the mother country has to offer. Castles, abbeys and stately homes in various stages of decay perforate a landscape of verdant valleys, bleak hill farms and rugged coastline on a virtual par with Scotland's most legendary landscapes. The capital boasts some cracking new satellite attractions, too, including the vast indoor climbing centre at Ratho and the boatlifting engineering marvel that is the Falkirk Wheel, while the large sculpture park at Jupiter Artland is an unexpected highlight of the region's irrepressible art scene.

South Queensferry & The Forth Bridges

MAP PAGE 130

8 miles northwest of Edinburgh city centre. From Edinburgh Waverley take the bi-hourly train to Dalmeny. From there, it's just under a mile to town, west on Station Road then turn right on The Loan.

Best known today for its location at the southern end of three mighty **Forth Bridges**, the small town of **South Queensferry** is an attractive old settlement, with its narrow, cobbled High Street lined by tightly packed old buildings. Through a gap, there's a great

Forth Rail Bridge

perspective of the Forth Bridges from the old stone harbour and curved, pebbly beach – the scene each New Year's Day of the teeth-chattering "Loony Dook", when a gaggle of hungover locals charges into the sea for the sharpest of dips.

While the final death knell for the ferry service from here to Fife – that had run since the eleventh century – rang on the opening of the first road bridge, there's still much local pride in the crossings that form the unavoidable backdrop to this town, as evidenced in the local museum on the High Street that detail their construction.

The bridges themselves, erected across three separate centuries, were each pioneering in its own right. The cantilevered **Forth Rail Bridge**, built from 1883 to 1890, ranks among the supreme achievements of Victorian engineering. Some 50,000 tons of steel were used in the construction of a design that manages to express grace as well as might.

Its neighbour, the **Forth Road Bridge** was the fourth-largest suspension bridge in the world on its completion in 1964. A combination of its gradual decay and the increased volumes of traffic led to the decision to build a new road bridge a little further to the west.

Jupiter Artland

Opened in 2017, **Queensferry Crossing** – the world's longest cable stayed bridge – with its white symmetrical cables gracefully fanning out from a trio of towers to the deck below, is as much admired for its restrained beauty as its engineering prowess.

The best way to admire all three engineering feats at once is to make use of the pedestrian and cycle lane on the Forth Road Bridge. In 2022, the Forth Bridges Trail, a five-mile circular route, was launched, connecting sixteen attractions in Queensferry and along the Forth Road Bridge – from the iconic bridge towers to *Hawes Inn*, which is immortalized in Robert Louis Stevenson's novel, *Kidnapped*. Along the way, you can discover historical facts and local stories while taking in scenic views of the bridges and the Firth of the Forth.

Jupiter Artland

MAP PAGE 130
Wilkieston, 11 miles west of Edinburgh on the B7015. www.jupiterartland.org. Charge. Bus #X27 from Princes Street.

Fulfilling the dreams of its art collector owners, this one-hundred-acre country pile has been transformed since the turn of the century into the remarkable sculpture park **Jupiter Artland**. Its appeal as a virgin project, an unparalleled blank canvas, has drawn in many of the heavyweights of outdoor installation like Charles Jencks, whose signature swirling grassy hillocks and ponds also feature outside Edinburgh's Modern Art Gallery. Here, his landscape entitled "Cells of Life" interprets the biological process of mitosis using large, grassy walnut whip-shaped mounds dissected by a drivable causeway. Andy Goldsworthy contributes a string of installations, too, including a complete drystone cottage and a clay tree while Sam Durant's *Scaffold*, a protest interpretation of a gallows, has an unlikely secondary function as a children's climbing frame.

Edinburgh International Climbing Arena (EICA)

MAP PAGE 130
South Platt Hill, Ratho. www.edinburgh leisure.co.uk. Charge. Take a tram westbound to Edinburgh Park and change onto bus #20 westbound. Alight at Ratho and walk for 2min west along the canal. By car, follow signs from the A8 westbound.

Europe's largest indoor climbing centre, the **Edinburgh**

DAY-TRIPS

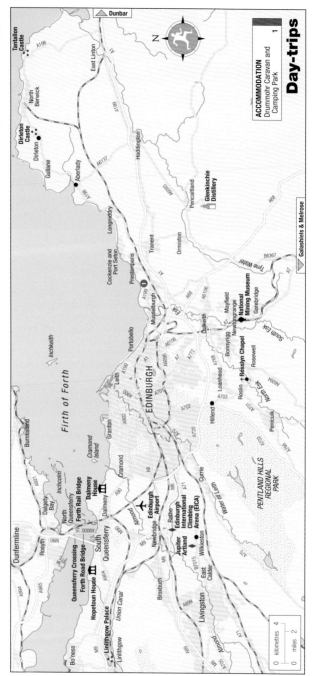

Day-trips

ACCOMMODATION
Drummohr Caravan and
Camping Park   1

International Climbing Arena (EICA) is built into the remnants of a disused quarry on the banks of the Union Canal. The place is truly gigantic and some of the climbs challenge not only your skills and stamina but also your head for heights. You'll need to bring a partner to belay with, and ideally that person will have completed a short belaying course. If you don't have your own harness, any necessary equipment can be bought or hired from the shop within the complex. For the kids' Clip and Climb course, belaying is automated. There are also a number of rope-free boulders on which you can practise specific techniques with a crash mat below to break your fall.

Dalmeny House

MAP PAGE 130

Dalmeny Estate, 3 miles east of Queensferry. www.dalmeny.co.uk. Charge. On foot, follow Queensferry High Street eastwards for 1.5 miles until you reach the estate entrance. By car, follow signposts from the A90 near Queensferry.

Set on a 2000-acre estate between South Queensferry and Cramond, this Tudor revivalist manor may not be the prettiest country seat you'll encounter in Scotland, but the quality of the items on show at **Dalmeny House** makes it a fascinating place to visit. As well as some of the finest Baroque and Neoclassical furniture produced for Louis' XIV, XV and XVI in the hundred years before the French Revolution, there's also a valuable selection of memorabilia relating to Napoleon Bonaparte. The art collection is surprisingly strong, too, with a very rare set of tapestries made from cartoons by Goya, and portraits by Raeburn, Reynolds, Gainsborough and Lawrence. Plans are underway to renovate the house, adding a new terrace and reimagining the space as accommodation, without compromising the integrity of the listed building.

Hopetoun House

Hopetoun House

MAP PAGE 130

Hopetoun Estate, 3 miles west of Queensferry. www.hopetoun.co.uk. Charge, free tour daily at 2pm. On foot, follow the coastline westwards from Queensferry for 3 miles; by car, take M90 turn-off onto the A904 and follow signs.

Sitting in its own extensive estate on the south shore of the Forth, **Hopetoun House** is one of the most impressive stately homes in Scotland. The original house was built at the turn of the eighteenth century for the first earl of Hopetoun by Sir William Bruce, the architect of Holyroodhouse. A couple of decades later, William Adam carried out an enormous extension, engulfing the structure with a curvaceous main facade and two projecting wings – superb examples of Roman Baroque pomp and swagger. Hopetoun's architecture is undoubtedly its most compelling feature, but the furnishings aren't completely overwhelmed, with some impressive seventeenth-century tapestries, Meissen porcelain and a distinguished collection of paintings, including portraits by Gainsborough, Ramsay and Raeburn. The house's grounds include a long, regal driveway and lovely walks along woodland trails and the banks of the Forth.

Inchcolm Island

MAP PAGE 130

Five miles northeast of South Queensferry near the Fife shore. From South Queensferry: Maid of the Forth, Hawes Pier. www.maidoftheforth.co.uk. £20 for 3hr landing trip. From Edinburgh's Waverley Bridge: Forth Boat Tours. www.forthtours. com. 3hr trip £20.

Home to the best-preserved medieval abbey in Scotland, **Inchcolm Island** was founded in 1235 after King Alexander I was stormbound here and took refuge in a hermit's cell. Although the structure is half-ruined today, the tower, octagonal chapterhouse and echoing cloisters are intact and well worth exploring. The hour and a half you're given ashore by the boat timetables also allows time for a picnic on the abbey's lawns or the chance to explore Inchcolm's old military fortifications and extensive bird-nesting grounds.

Linlithgow Palace

MAP PAGE 130

Kirkgate, Linlithgow, just off the M9 motorway. By train: 4 hourly; 20min.

www.historicenvironment.scot. Charge; HES.

Linlithgow Palace is a splendid fifteenth-century ruin, romantically poised on the edge of Linlithgow Loch and associated with some of Scotland's best-known historical figures, including Mary, Queen of Scots, who was born here on December 8, 1542 and became queen six days later. A royal manor house is believed to have existed on this site since the time of David I, though James I began construction of the present palace, a process that continued through two centuries and the reign of no fewer than eight monarchs. From the top of the northwest tower, Queen Margaret looked out in vain for the return of James IV from the field of Flodden in 1513 – indeed, the views from her bower, six storeys up from the ground, are exceptional. The ornate octagonal fountain in the inner courtyard, with its wonderfully intricate figures and medallion heads, flowed with wine for the wedding of James V and Mary of Guise.

Rosslyn Chapel

MAP PAGE 130

Linlithgow Palace

Chapel Loan, Roslin, 7 miles south of Edinburgh just off the A701. www.rosslyn chapel.com. Charge. Bus #15 westbound from Princes Street in Edinburgh.

As much revered for its sublime stone carvings – some of the finest in the world – as its alleged crusader connections, **Rosslyn Chapel** is more cathedral-like in its dimensions. It was intended to be a huge collegiate church dedicated to St Matthew, but construction halted soon after the founder's death in 1484, and the vestry built onto the facade nearly four hundred years later is the sole subsequent addition.

Rosslyn's exterior bristles with pinnacles, gargoyles, flying buttresses and canopies, while inside the **stonework** is, if anything, even more intricate. The foliage carving is particularly outstanding, with botanically accurate depictions of over a dozen different leaves and plants. Among them are cacti and Indian corn, compounding the legend that the founder's grandfather, the daring sea adventurer Prince Henry of Orkney, did indeed set foot in the New World a century before Columbus. The rich and subtle figurative sculptures have given Rosslyn the nickname of "a bible in stone", though they're more allegorical than literal, with portrayals of the Dance of Death, the Seven Acts of Mercy and the Seven Deadly Sins.

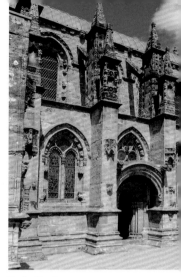

Rosslyn Chapel

National Mining Museum

MAP PAGE 130
8 miles southeast of Edinburgh on the A7, Lady Victoria Colliery, Newtongrange. www.nationalminingmuseum.com. Charge for tours. Trains run from Edinburgh Waverley to Newtongrange every 30min (22min); by bus, #29 & #33 from Princes Street southbound.

Closed in 1989, this Victorian colliery, now the **National Mining Museum**, is one of the best preserved in the world. A variety of exhibits show numerous engineering innovations throughout the years, including the largest steam engine in Scotland, originally used to haul men up and down the pit shaft. The site is truly vast and much of the colliery will remain in the renovation queue for years to come, giving the place an atmospheric ambiance of decay. Ex-minor tour guides offer real insight into what it was like to work here while you absorb the sights, smells and sounds of the working pit.

Pentland Hills

MAP PAGE 130
Buses #4 and #15 westbound from Princes Street will take you to Hillend at the foot of the hills.

The **Pentland Hills**, a chain some eighteen miles long and five miles wide, dominate most views south of Edinburgh and offer walkers and mountain bikers a thrilling taste of wild Scottish countryside just beyond the suburbs.

The simplest way to get a taste of the scenery of the Pentlands is to set off from the car park by the ski centre at **Hillend**, at the northeast end of the range; take the path up the right-hand side of the dry ski slopes, turning left shortly

The Pentland Hills

after crossing a stile to reach a prominent point with outstanding views over Edinburgh and Fife.

Glenkinchie Distillery

MAP PAGE 130

7 miles southwest of Haddinton on the A6093, turn south at Pencaitland onto Lempockwells Road and follow the signs for two miles. A shuttle bus connects the distillery to Waterloo Place in the city centre (charge); seats booked by phone 01875 342 012, www.malts.com. Charge.

The **Glenkinchie Distillery** is the closest place outside of Edinburgh where the uisce beatha – the water of life – is produced. Here, of course, it emphasizes the qualities that set Glenkinchie, a lighter, drier malt, apart from the peaty, smoky whiskies of the north and west. On display, there's a pleasant little exhibition featuring some quaint distilling relics, which enhances the factory tour experience almost as much as the free dram finale.

Melrose and its Abbey

MAP PAGE 130

37 miles southeast of Edinburgh. 0131 668 8600. Charge; HES. By car, follow the A7 south to Galashiels then take A6091. By train, Edinburgh to Tweedbank every 30min; 55min. Take a taxi or bus link for the last two miles to Melrose.

Tucked in between the River Tweed and the gorse-backed Eildon Hills, minuscule **Melrose** is one of the most appealing towns in the Borders. Centred on its busy little market square, its narrow streets are trimmed by a harmonious ensemble of styles, from pretty little cottages and tweedy shops to high-standing Georgian and Victorian facades.

Its chief draw is the twelfth-century pink- and red-tinted stone ruins of **Melrose Abbey** that soar above their riverside surroundings (abbey church is currently closed for masonry inspections).

Legend has it that the heart of Robert I is buried at Melrose Abbey (his body having been buried at Dunfermline Abbey), and in 1997, when a heart cask was publicly exhumed, this theory received an unexpected boost.

North Berwick

MAP PAGE 130

24 miles east of Edinburgh. By car, follow the A1 from Edinburgh until the junction for A198. Trains run hourly from Waverley Station (33min). Boat trips to Bass Rock from the Scottish Seabird Centre: Harbour Lodge, 7 Beach Road. www.seabird.org. Charge.

North Berwick has a great deal of charm and a somewhat faded, old-fashioned air, its guesthouses and hotels strung along the shore in all their Victorian and Edwardian sobriety. The town's small harbour is set on a headland that cleaves two crescents of golden sand, providing the town with an attractive coastal setting. Foodies are beginning to follow the culinary trail to North Berwick, lured by the independent coffee shops littering the cobblestone streets – *Steampunk Roastery* is a must – and by sea-to-plate haunts like the *Lobster Shack* (www.lobstershack.co.uk) dishing up soul-nourishing plates of fish tacos, lobster rolls and seafood chowder from its harbourfront food truck. A short distance offshore, the Bass Rock rises vertiginously from the sea and gives the town its defining characteristic. Described by David Attenborough as "one of the twelve wonders of the world", the small island is home to 150,000 gannets that thrill boat trippers with their diving raids on the choppy waters below.

Tantallon Castle

MAP PAGE 130
3 miles east of North Berwick on the A198. 01620 892 727. Charge; HES. From North Berwick, take the Dunbar bus (Eves Coaches #120; Mon–Sat 6 daily, 2 on Sun; 6 min); on foot, you can walk there from town along the cliffs in around an hour.
The melodramatic ruins of the fourteenth-century **Tantallon Castle** stand on the precipitous cliffs facing the Bass Rock. With a sheer drop down to the sea on three sides and a sequence of moats and ditches on the fourth, the castle's desolate invincibility is daunting, especially when the wind howls over the remaining battlements and the surf crashes on the rocks far below. However, the castle's vulnerability on its precarious perch has come to the fore and it is currently closed to the public (grounds open) as masonry work on the historic edifice is underway; check the website for date of reopening.

Dirleton Castle

MAP PAGE 130
2.5 miles west of North Berwick signposted off the A198. 01620 850 330. Charge; HES. First Bus #124 from the High Street in North Berwick (Mon–Sun every half hour; 15min).
The genteel hamlet of **Dirleton** huddles around its romantic thirteenth-century ruin that saw action in the Wars of Scottish Independence. It was later rendered militarily defunct after a besiegement by Oliver Cromwell's army to flush out bandits. Today, it's an attractive relic, largely intact, though it is currently closed for a masonry survey (check the website for updates). The restored Victorian

gardens remain open, as do the exhibition and shop.

Dunbar

MAP PAGE 130
30 miles east of Edinburgh. By train every 30 to 60min; 25min. By car, follow the A1 east from Edinburgh. John Muir's Birthplace: 126 High St. www.jmbt.org.uk. Free.
The coastal town of **Dunbar**, with its delightfully intricate double harbour set beside the shattered remains of a once-mighty castle, is today best known globally as the birthplace of nineteenth-century explorer and naturalist, John Muir (1838–1914), who created the United States' national park system. Muir spent his formative years here growing up in one of grand old stone buildings, now a free museum, that grace the recently spruced-up High Street.

While Muir might have left for America, the remaining townspeople were left to make a living from the choppy North Sea and while today's inhabitants are more likely to be city-bound commuters than fisher-folk, the town's new-found destination as a surfing hotspot is keeping the place ticking over.

Dunbar harbour

ACCOMMODATION

The Old Rectory Suite at The Witchery Apartments

Accommodation

Already a tourism hotspot, Edinburgh's recent upsurge in visitor numbers has seen the number of hotels and aparthotels in the city grow exponentially. This, together with Airbnb's seemingly irrepressible march, has resulted in a bewildering choice of places to stay in the city. Bargains are always there to be found, usually by way of a last-minute booking or via a promotions agency and if you're on a really tight budget, there are plenty of hostels, particularly around the Old Town. Making reservations is worthwhile at any time of year, and is strongly recommended for stays during the Festival and around Hogmanay, when prices swell considerably and spaces get booked months in advance.

Old Town

APEX GRASSMARKET MAP PAGE 56. 31–35 Grassmarket. www.apexhotels.co.uk. This ex-university building turned 175-bed business-oriented hotel has comfortable rooms, some with unencumbered views to the Castle and balconies that peer down onto Grassmarket below. Up top, there's a double-rosette rooftop restaurant with a dramatic skyline view – especially after dark – while downstairs you'll find a small pool and gym. ££££

IBIS EDINBURGH CENTRE MAP PAGE 38. 6 Hunter Square. www.ibis.com. Probably the best-located chain hotel cheapie in the Old Town, within sight of the Royal Mile; rooms are modern and inexpensive, but there are few facilities other than a rather plain bar. £££

MOTEL ONE – EDINBURGH ROYAL MAP PAGE 38. 18–21 Market St. www.motel-one.com. Located between the Old and New Towns and across from the station, this modern hotel cheapie is an ideal base for exploring the city. The best rooms have views onto Princes Street Gardens, as does the hotel's spacious bar. ££

RADISSON BLU HOTEL MAP PAGE 38. High St. www.radissonhotels.com. Spacious, purpose-built hotel with a gym, spa, pool, bar and restaurant. The sleek, modern rooms and public areas contrast with its sympathetically neo-medieval exterior. ££££

TRAVELODGE EDINBURGH CENTRAL MAP PAGE 38. 33 St Mary's St. www.travelodge.co.uk. There's more than a hint of concrete brutalism in the look of

Accommodation price codes

Each accommodation reviewed in this Guide is accompanied by a price category, based on the cost of a standard double room in high season. Price ranges don't include breakfast, unless stated otherwise. For hostels, dormitory bed prices are indicated as well as private rooms.

£ = under £75
££ = £75–120
£££ = £120–175
££££ = over £175

this chain hotel, but it's well priced and centrally located, 100 yards from the Royal Mile near some excellent restaurants. At weekends it tends to fill up with stag and hen parties, but the rooms are quiet enough if a little grungy. ££

THE WITCHERY APARTMENTS MAP PAGE 38. Castlehill. www.thewitchery.com. Nine riotously indulgent suites grouped around this famously spooky restaurant just downhill from the castle; expect antique furniture, big leather armchairs, tapestry-draped beds, oak panelling and huge rolltop baths, as well as ultramodern sound systems and complimentary champagne. ££££

Southside

94DR MAP PAGE 124. 94 Dalkeith Rd. www.94dr.com. A boutique guesthouse offering three different styles with its couture, bespoke and tailored rooms. Front-facing ones have a view of Arthur's Seat. £££

POLLOCK HALLS OF RESIDENCE, UNIVERSITY OF EDINBURGH MAP PAGE 124. 18 Holyrood Park Rd. www.edinburgh first.com. Unquestionably the best setting of any of the city's university accommodation, right beside Holyrood Park, just southeast of the Old Town. It provides single rooms, doubles and self-catering flats, mostly available Easter & June to mid-Sept, though some rooms are available year-round. **Singles/doubles £; flats ££££/week**

TEN HILL PLACE MAP PAGE 56. 10 Hill Place. www.tenhillplace.com. A contemporary, efficient hotel linked to the historic Royal College of Surgeons, with 78 sleek and smartly styled bedrooms, all run according to an environmentally conscious policy. £££

New Town

ARDENLEE GUEST HOUSE MAP PAGE 102. 9 Eyre Place. www.ardenlee-guest-house.edinburgh-hotel.org. Welcoming guesthouse at the foot of the New Town, with original Victorian features and nine reasonably spacious rooms, seven of which are en suite and some suitable for families. ££

EDEN LOCKE MAP PAGE 86. 127 George St. www.lockeliving.com. Hotels for hipsters; *Eden Locke* offers on-trend Gryzwinski and Pons-designed aparthotel studios with corner sofas and curated artworks. The kitchens are small but somehow fit in a washer-dryer and dishwasher, while the bathroom comes with Apothecary skin products and a rubber duck. £££

GERALD'S PLACE MAP PAGE 86. 21b Abercromby Place. www.geraldsplace. com. A homely taste of New Town life at an upmarket but hospitable and comfy basement B&B. The rustic decor is tasteful, with some fine artwork and old books to catch your eye, while the breakfasts are generous, with many home-made components. £££

THE GLASSHOUSE MAP PAGE 86. 2 Greenside Place. www.theglasshousehotel. co.uk. Incorporating the castellated facade of the former Lady Glenorchy's Church, this ultra-hip hotel has 65 chichi rooms with push-button curtains and sliding doors opening onto a huge, lush roof garden scattered with Philippe Starck furniture. Perfect if you're in town for a weekend of indulgence. ££££

GLENEAGLES TOWNHOUSE MAP PAGE 76. 39 St Andrew Sq. www.gleneagles. com/townhouse. The much-anticipated Edinburgh outpost of the iconic *Gleneagles Hotel* features 33 elegant rooms decked out in chic country style; a luxury spa offering Barbara Sturm and Tata Harper treatments; *The Spence* restaurant; and a members-only rooftop bar. Very exclusive, luxe feel – and a price tag to match. ££££

THE GUEST ROOM MAP PAGE 86. 31a Nelson St. 0131 556 4798. A notably unobtrusive B&B offering two spacious rooms with a choice of courtyard or garden views. Start the day with a breakfast tray of berries, porridge and freshly squeezed orange. £££

HOLIDAY INN EXPRESS EDINBURGH CITY CENTRE MAP PAGE 86. Picardy Place. www.ihg.com. It's by a busy roundabout, but otherwise in a good location in an elegant old Georgian tenement near the top of Broughton St, with 161 rooms featuring neat but predictable chain-hotel decor and facilities. **££££**

INTERCONTINENTAL MAP PAGE 86. 19–21 George St. www.edinburgh. intercontinental.com. A beautiful example of a prime Georgian building, inside and out, thanks to its Neoclassical frontage and sympathetically harmonious decor. The suites are luxurious from top to tail and often come with lofty views north to the Firth of Forth. **££££**.

NIRA CALEDONIA MAP PAGE 102. 6 Gloucester Place. www.niracaledonia.com. Elegant and comfortable townhouse hotel located on a typical New Town terrace. Decor is modern, opulent and striking, if a little overwhelming. **££££**

RABBLE MAP PAGE 86. 55a Frederick St. www.rabbleedinburgh.co.uk. Ten much-sought-after rooms at the back of the popular New Town bar and restaurant. Beautifully styled with beds fitted with walnut headboards and plush fabrics, they look out onto a cobbled lane behind. **££££**

REGENT HOUSE MAP PAGE 86. 3 Forth St, Broughton. www.regenthousehotel. co.uk. A good-value small hotel over four floors that makes up for its lack of glamour with a great location, right in the heart of Broughton on a quiet side street. Some rooms are big enough to accommodate three to five people. **££**

ROCK HOUSE MAP PAGE 76. 28 Calton Hill. www.rockhouse-edinburgh.com. A trio of exquisite holiday let properties just one minute's walk from Princes Street, yet in an improbable village-like setting on Calton Hill's western incline. *Rock House* was built in the 1750s; a delightful orange lime-wash frontage surrounding a formal water garden with a converted octagonal photographer's studio to the side. The two buildings – divided into three units, with log fires, William Morris paper and muddy green sofas – balance taste and luxury to perfection. **££££**

ROOMZZZ APARTHOTEL MAP PAGE 76. St James Quarter. www.roomzzz.com. A cluster of 74 brand-new apartments in St James Quarter, with a shared outdoor terrace overlooking the city. All come with king-size beds, super-fast wi-fi and a kitchenette; the best (and most expensive) come with oodles of space and a private balcony. **££££**

TIGERLILY MAP PAGE 86. 125 George St. www.tigerlilyedinburgh.co.uk. A glitzy boutique hotel, bar and restaurant that epitomizes the excess of twenty-first-century George Street. A classic Georgian townhouse transformed into a flamboyant design extravaganza; indulgent pink or black bedroom suites are kitted out with decadent fabrics and some even have a real fire. **££££**

W HOTEL MAP PAGE 76. St James Quarter. www.whotel.com-edinburgh.com. The swanky *W Hotel* brand is coming to Scotland with its 2023 opening in St James Quarter. The striking architecture is dividing opinions, with some nicknaming the spiralling design poking above New Town's rooftops as "Edinburgh's poo". Expect 12 floors of sleek rooms wending up to a rooftop bar, an outdoor terrace and *Sushi Samba*, a Japanese, Brazilian and Peruvian fusion restaurant with an original outpost in London. **££££**

Leith and North Edinburgh

MALMAISON MAP PAGE 108. 1 Tower Place. www.malmaison.com. Chic, modern hotel set in the grand old seamen's hostel just back from the wharf-side. Bright, bold original designs in each room, plus a gym, room service, Parisian brasserie and café-bar serving lighter meals. **££££**

Hostels

A&O EDINBURGH CITY MAP PAGE 38. 50 Blackfriars St. www.aohostels.com. An upmarket hostel just off the Royal Mile, offering 131 spacious and comfortable rooms – singles, doubles, family and multi-bed sleeping up to six – each with its own shower and toilet. ££

ARGYLE BACKPACKERS MAP PAGE 124. 14 Argyle Place, Marchmont. www.argyle-backpackers.co.uk. A quiet, less intense version of the typical backpackers' hostel, pleasantly located in three adjoining townhouses near the Meadows park in studenty Marchmont, just south of the Old Town. The dorms are small – up to 6 beds per room – and there are a dozen or so twin rooms as well as a communal conservatory and garden at the back. £

CASTLE ROCK HOSTEL MAP PAGE 56. 15 Johnston Terrace. www.castlerockedinburgh.com. Tucked below the Castle ramparts, with two hundred or so beds arranged in large, bright dorms, as well as triple and quads and some doubles. The communal areas include a games room with pool and table tennis plus a sunny patio. £

EDINBURGH CENTRAL SYHA MAP PAGE 86. 9 Haddington Place. www.syha.org.uk. In a handy location at the top of Leith Walk (a 5min stroll from the centre), this five-star hostel has single, double and triple private rooms as well as eight-bed dorms with en-suite facilities. There is a reasonably priced bistro in addition to self-catering kitchen facilities. **Private rooms ££; dorms £**

HIGH STREET HOSTEL MAP PAGE 38. 8 Blackfriars St. www.highstreethostel.com. Lively and popular hostel in an attractive sixteenth-century building just off the Royal Mile, with dorms of up to 18 beds and twin rooms. The communal facilities include a kitchen, a quiet room and a large party dining lounge with piano and pool table. **Twin rooms ££; dorms £**

KICK ASS HOSTELS MAP PAGE 56. 2 West Port. www.kickasshostels.co.uk. With its own in-house café and pub, and segregated dorms some of which have a clear view up to the castle, this is a year-round popular stop attracting a young crowd. The rooms sleep up to 12 and have USB power points, lockers and electronic swipe cards. £

STAY CENTRAL HOTEL MAP PAGE 56. 139 Cowgate. www.staycentral.co.uk. A popular option for large stag and hen groups, this neoteric hotel has lots of rooms that sleep up to six, including the 'Ultimate Party Room' with table tennis, a dart board and a big fridge. If you're partying hard, the hotel can arrange for a booze delivery and a live DJ set in your room. ££££

Campsites

DRUMMOHR CARAVAN AND CAMPING PARK MAP PAGE 130. Levenhall, Musselburgh, on the B1348. www.drummohr.org. A large, pleasant site on the eastern edge of Musselburgh, a coastal satellite town to the east of Edinburgh, with excellent transport connections to the city centre. As well as the usual pitches, there are a few "bothies" (basic wooden huts that sleep up to four), and the more luxurious lodges that sleep up to six. **Camping/bothies £; lodges £££**

EDINBURGH CARAVAN CLUB MAP PAGE 115. Site 35 Marine Drive, Silverknowes, 5 miles northwest of the centre. www.caravanclub.co.uk. Caravan-dominated site in a pleasant location close to the shoreline, though there's little else here. Cramond village is a 10min walk west along the shore and has a pub and cafés. £

ESSENTIALS

Princes Street

Arrival

Edinburgh is well served by its busy and central Waverley train station as well as its ever-growing airport seven miles to the west. Fast becoming a burgeoning international hub, the city now sees flights taxi in from China, the US, Canada, UAE and Mexico as well as numerous European cities. Edinburgh's train, tram and bus terminals are within walking distance of each other in the heart of the city.

By plane

Travel from Edinburgh **airport** to the city centre is fast and economical by bus or tram.

Edinburgh

Edinburgh Airport (www.edinburgh airport.com) lies around seven miles west of the city centre, just off the M8 and M9 motorways. The cheapest and often quickest way into town is by **bus**, most conveniently on the Airlink #100 (24hr; journey 20–45min), departing from Domestic Arrivals (Stance D), and terminating at Waverley Bridge, just outside Edinburgh Waverley train station (see page 145). Services run every 30min between 1am and 4.30am and then every 10min between 4.30am and 1am, with tickets priced at £5.50 (£2.75 child) single and £8 (£4 child) open return. If you're staying in Leith, you might want to take the Skylink #200 service (changes to #N22 through the night; Stance D), departing from Stance B and with timetable and ticket prices broadly similar, though the journey can take almost an hour at peak times. Tickets for both Airlink and Skylink service can be bought at the kiosk outside Domestic Arrivals, though it's easier to pay in cash on board and – unlike most city buses – change is given. For detailed route and timetable information on all services, see www. lothianbuses.co.uk/airport. If you

fancy travelling in a little more style, the **tram** (www.edinburghtrams.com) runs from the airport to Princes Street (daily 6.26am–11.19pm, every 7–10min; journey 31min) and costs £7.50 (£3.80 child) single, £9.50 (£6 child) return. Tickets are available from the machines on the platform. You can also buy tickets for the tram and all airport bus services via the Transport for Edinburgh mobile app (see page 146). Both metered **taxis** and fixed-price private hire from the airport to the city centre cost upwards of £25, with a journey time of around 20min depending on traffic. Capital Cars (0131 777 7777, www.capitalcars scotland.co.uk) offers a meet-and-greet service for an additional £17.50.

Glasgow

Glasgow Airport (www.glasgowairport. com) lies around eight miles west of Glasgow city centre, near Paisley. The 24hr Glasgow Airport Express #500 **bus** service (every 10min; journey 25min), is the fastest option for onward transport to the city centre, departing from Stance 1, stopping at Queen Street train station (for onward train travel to Edinburgh) and terminating at Buchanan Street bus station (for onward coach travel to Edinburgh). Tickets are priced at £10 single and £16 open return. **Taxis** cost upwards of £25 to the city centre, depending on traffic. In terms of journey time and frequency, there's not much to choose between bus and train when thinking about **onward travel** to Edinburgh; both depart every 10–15min during the day and take around 1hr 10–20min. Citylink (www.citylink.co.uk) is the main coach operator; services run frequently throughout the day and night (check website for times), with some of those services stopping at Edinburgh airport. Trains (www.scotrail.co.uk) are significantly more expensive and can get very crowded at peak times, often with standing room only.

By train and coach

Arriving by train from elsewhere in Britain (or the south of Scotland), your service will terminate in Edinburgh Waverley (www.networkrail.co.uk/stations/edinburgh-waverley) at the east end of Princes Street, served by most city bus routes. If arriving from Glasgow or the north, your service will first make a stop at the city's other main station, Haymarket, useful if you're staying in the West End. Travelling by **bus** or **coach** from elsewhere in either Britain (www.nationalexpress.com) or Scotland (www.citylink.co.uk), you'll arrive in the terminal next to St Andrew Square near the east end of Princes Street, a 2min walk from Waverley.

Getting around

Although Edinburgh occupies a large area relative to its population (just over half a million people), most places worth visiting lie within the compact city centre, which is easily explored on foot or by bike. There's nevertheless a generally efficient – if often congested – **public transport network**, consisting for the most part of buses, with many services terminating on, or passing through (or near), Princes Street, the city's main thoroughfare. Though it's unlikely you'll need it for most journeys, the bus station is located just north of here off the corner of St Andrew Square.

Buses

The city is fairly well served by buses; by far the largest majority of these are the iconic maroon double-deckers operated by **Lothian Buses** (www.lothianbuses.com), and all services referred to in the Guide are run by Lothian, unless otherwise stated. All services are numbered and most run at a daytime frequency of 10–20min. A reduced network of **night buses** also operates, with departures every hour or so (every 10min on some services at weekends) and with their route numbers prefixed by 'N'. Every bus stop displays maps indicating which services frequent it and the routes they take;

Tramspotting

Almost as infamous as Irvine Welsh's novel, and doubtless having clocked up even more column inches, Edinburgh's hugely controversial **tram project** finally reached completion in 2014 after almost six highly fraught years. At long last, Edinburgh Airport had a **modern rail link** to the city centre. The end product may have been two and a half lines short, suffered a chaotic construction that pushed the patience of the good citizens of Edinburgh to breaking point, coming in over double its initial budget, but the solitary 14km of line that finally emerged has confounded critics by turning a profit two years ahead of schedule and exceeding passenger targets. In the wake of its surprising success, after yet more discussion and delay, Edinburgh Council gave the green light to extend the line to Newhaven as originally planned. Today, services trundle into Ocean Terminal and Newhaven (daily 6.26am–11.42pm, every 7–10min; journey time), costing £2 (£1 child) single, £3.80 return (£1.90 child).

an increasing number also have live departure information. Single **fares** are priced at £2 (£1 child) (£4.50 for night buses) and the easiest way to pay is in cash as you board, though no change is issued so you'll need the exact coinage. Contactless payment is also possible as you board but bizarrely not for child fares. Other options include a day ticket (£5 adult, £2.50 child) or a family day ticket for up to 2 adults and 3 children (£10.50), both allowing unlimited travel on bus or tram. For the longer term, a Ridacard pass (£22) allows a week's unlimited travel on bus (including night services) and tram services. Ridacards and indeed any tickets can be bought from the Lothian Bus Travelhubs at 31 Waverley Bridge (Mon–Sat 8.30am–5.30pm); or 49 Shandwick Place (same hours). You might also want to download the Transport for Edinburgh app (see box). For an excellent map of the entire network, see www.lothian buses.com.

The predominantly white, single-decker buses of First Edinburgh (www. firstgroup.com) run services on a number of the main routes through the city, but are better for outlying towns and villages. It has its own system of tickets and day tickets, similar in structure to Lothian Buses, though drivers will always give change. Most services depart from or near the main bus station at St Andrew Square.

Trams
While you may well use Edinburgh's solitary **tram line** (www.edinburgh trams.com) to get to and from the airport, it's fairly unlikely you'll use it for much else, serving as it does largely suburban and commuter destinations in the city's far west. The terminal is on York Place in the New Town, just behind the bus station. Services depart every 7min daily from 6am to midnight, with a single ticket (excluding the airport) costing £2 for adults and £1 for children; Lothian Buses day passes (see page 145) and Ridacards (see page 145) are also valid. Tram tickets must be purchased from the ticket machines prior to boarding; credit and debit cards accepted.

Cycling
Although hilly, Edinburgh is a reasonably bike-friendly city, with a growing number of **cycle paths** particularly around the suburbs where disused railway lines and waterway paths form the backbone of the network. The new City Centre West to East Link (CCWEL) connecting Roseburn and Leith Walk, via Haymarket and the West End, aims to tackle the poor cycling infrastructure in the city centre. Started in February 2022, the £19.4 million project is set to complete in mid-2023, though the project has been long-delayed. Future plans include a new George Street cycle path. Local biking advocacy group Spokes publishes an excellent map of the city with recommended cycle routes; pick up a copy at the tourist office. Bikes can be hired from Cycle Scotland, 29 Blackfriars St (from £25/

Transport for Edinburgh app
The free **Transport for Edinburgh mobile app** (www.tfeapp.com) allows you to buy bundles of electronic tickets for both bus and tram, particularly useful if you'll be making single bus trips on various days, but not enough to justify a Ridacard – minimum spend is £22, and you'll also be able to access live departure info for every bus route in the city.

day; www.cyclescotland.co.uk). The company also offers scenic guided city **cycle tours** (daily 11am; £35/person; e-bike option available for £50), taking in the likes of Holyrood Park, Arthur's Seat, the *Sheep Heid Inn* (see page 73), Dr Neil's Garden (see page 71) and Craigmillar Castle (see page 71).

Taxis

Edinburgh is well endowed with **taxi ranks**, and you can also hail black cabs on the street. All taxis are metered, and costs (set by the council) are. Companies include Central Taxis (0131 229 2468, www.taxis-edinburgh. co.uk) and City Cabs (0131 228 1211, www.citycabs.co.uk). Uber (www.uber. com) users will have little trouble finding a ride, either.

Sightseeing tours and guided walks

Year round, a fleet of state-of-the-art **open-top double-deckers** run by Edinburgh Bus Tours (www.edinburgh tour.com; daily roughly 9am–6pm; every 10–15min (every 30min Oct– March); 1hr; £16) lines up on Waverley Bridge, hoovering up the tourists pouring out of Waverley Station and the

Airlink bus (see page 144). Several themed tours are available covering most of the major sights, as well as Three Bridges option (see page 128) combined with a cruise on the Firth of Forth (3.5hr; £30). Unsurprisingly for such an atmospheric city, Edinburgh is served by countless **walking** tours. As well as traditional historical tours (for which the family-run Edinburgh Guided Tour has one of the best reputations: www.edinburghguided tour.com), there are myriad – and often highly acclaimed – specialist variations covering almost every conceivable theme from the inevitable ghosts to Harry Potter (www.potter trail.com), gourmet food and drink (www.eatwalkedinburgh.co.uk), small-group photography (www.james christiephotography.com) and, of course, Outlander (www.mercattours. com). Tours last anything from an hour or two to a whole day, and while many are priced in the £10–30 range, some of the specialist ones can cost double that. If you're on a budget, opt for one of the numerous cheap and cheerful free tours (www.edinburgh freetour.com, www.neweuropetours.eu/ edinburgh).

Directory A–Z

Accessible travel

Edinburgh is an old city; installing ramps, lifts, wide doorways and accessible toilets is, unfortunately, impossible in many of the city's older and historic buildings. Access has improved, however, with some of the city's most iconic attractions – including Edinburgh Castle (see page 36), the Palace of Holyrood House (see page 66) and the Scottish Parliament (see page 68) – relatively accessible. Some hotels and a handful of B&Bs have one or two adapted rooms, usually on the ground

floor and with step-free showers, grab rails and wider doorways.

Most **trains** in Scotland have wheelchair lifts, and assistance is, in theory, available at all manned stations – see www.scotrail.co.uk/plan-your-journey/accessible-travel. Wheelchair-users (alone or with a companion) and blind or partially sighted people (with a companion only) are automatically given thirty to fifty percent reductions on train fares. For more information and advice, contact the disability charity Capability Scotland (www.capability-scotland.org.uk).

Addresses

Edinburgh addresses come with postcodes at the end, consisting of the letters EH and a number giving the geographical location of the street in relation to the city. A further number and two letters specifies its location more precisely. Note that these numbers don't correspond to the actual distance from the centre.

Children, travelling with

Edinburgh is a great place for children and needn't necessarily put parents under undue financial strain, especially if they make use of the city's numerous parks and gardens. Public transport is free for under-6s and all major museums and galleries can be visited free of charge. Kids are generally welcomed in cafés and restaurants, but less so in pubs where there's usually a child policy notice at the entrance.

Costs

Edinburgh is by far the most **expensive** city in Scotland and among the priciest short-break destinations in the UK. A plunging pound in the wake of Brexit, which never fully recovered, has nevertheless eased costs for foreign visitors at least. The minimum expenditure for a couple staying at hostels, self-catering and eating the odd meal out is around £80–90 each per day. Staying at budget B&Bs, eating at unpretentious restaurants and visiting the odd tourist attraction, means spending at least £100 each per day. If you're renting a car, staying in comfortable B&Bs or hotels and eating well, you should reckon on at least £130 a day per person.

Crime

Edinburgh is a generally safe city, though should you have anything stolen or be involved in an incident that requires reporting, dial 101 from any location; 999 should only be used in emergencies – in other words, if someone is in immediate danger or a crime is taking place.

Electricity

Electricity supply in Edinburgh conforms to the EU standard of approximately 230V. Sockets are designed for British **three-pin plugs**, which are different from those in Europe and North America. Some tourist shops and central supermarkets will sell adaptors.

Embassies and consulates

Consulate General of Ireland, 16 Randolph Crescent (0131 226 7711, www.dfa.ie/irish-consulate/edinburgh); US Consulate, 3 Regent Terrace (0131 556 8315, http://uk.usembassy.gov/embassy-consulates/edinburgh).

Football

While the rivalry between Edinburgh's two footballing giants **Hearts** (www.heartsfc.co.uk) and **Hibernian** (www.hibernianfc.co.uk), might not be quite as fierce as Glasgow's Old Firm (Rangers and Celtic), it's near enough. Both clubs have suffered relegation from the **Premiership** in recent seasons (with Hearts having additionally faced administration), yet both have come roaring back to the top flight. Hibernian (aka Hibs) afforded the eastern half of the city one of its noisiest and most cathartic weekend-long celebrations in 2016, when they notched up a memorable victory over Rangers in the Scottish Cup, lifting the trophy for the first time since 1902. **Tickets** for home games are reasonably priced at around £25–35 and are normally available for sale via the clubs' respective websites.

Health

For minor ailments, pharmacists, known as **chemists** in Scotland, can dispense a limited range of drugs without a doctor's prescription. Most chemists are open standard shop hours (9am–5.30/6pm), though the "duty chemist" system obliges some to open late on a rotated basis.

In the event of an emergency, you can either turn up at the **Accident and Emergency** (A&E) department of Edinburgh's Royal Infirmary (0131 536 1000) on the southern edge of the city at 51 Little France Crescent, Old Dalkeith Road; or phone for an ambulance (999). A&E services are free to all. For non-emergency health concerns, you can phone the NHS 111 service (calls are free); they can let you know the nearest place for treatment, including for dental emergencies.

Internet

Practically all accommodation in Edinburgh offers **free wi-fi** as standard and public wi-fi is widespread in cafes, public transport etc. If you don't have your own smartphone, laptop or tablet, try the cheap or free internet access provided by most public libraries.

Left luggage

There are left luggage facilities at Edinburgh Airport, East Terminal (0330 223 0893; daily 4.30am–midnight); Glasgow Airport, Main Terminal (0330 223 0893; daily 5am–8pm); Edinburgh Waverley station, Platform 19 (0131 558 3829; daily 7am–11pm); Glasgow Queen Street station, near North Hannover Street entrance (0141 335 3276; daily 7am–10pm); Edinburgh bus station has storage lockers (24hr); Glasgow bus station, main Concourse (www.spt.co.uk).

LGBTQ+ travellers

Edinburgh's annual **Pride march** (www.prideedinburgh.org) is held in mid-June, with a parade from the Scottish Parliament through the Old Town. Broughton Street, Greenside Place and Picardy Place together form the "Pink Triangle", long the locus of the Edinburgh scene, with numerous bars and clubs. In 2021, The Gayborhood Foundation, an organization that recognizes leading gay areas around the world, dubbed Broughton Street a 'Gayborhood' – an enclave with a high population of LGBTQ+ residents, a dedication to LGBTQ+ rights and a proud support for the LGBTQ+ community. The website www.lgbtyouth.org.uk is a useful resource for younger people, while LGBT Health & Wellbeing (www.lgbt health.org.uk) operates a helpline four days a week (Tues–Thurs noon–9pm, Sun 1–6pm; 0800 464 7000).

Lost property

There are lost property units at Edinburgh Airport, East Terminal (0330 223 0893) and Glasgow Airport, Main Terminal (0330 223 0893). For train stations, contact Edinburgh Waverley, Platform 19 (0330 024 0215; Mon–Fri

Public holidays

You'll find all banks and most offices **closed** on the following days, while everything else pretty much runs to a **Sunday schedule** (except on Christmas Day, Boxing Day, New Year's Day and January 2 when everything shuts down): Good Friday (late March/April); Easter Monday (late March/April); first and last Mondays in May; first Monday in August. Note that the second Monday in April and third Monday in September are officially public holidays in Edinburgh, though many businesses – and often public offices – remain open.

9am–5.30pm) or Glasgow Queen Street's lost property near the North Hannover Street entrance (0141 335 3276; Mon–Sat 7am–10pm). For property left on long-distance buses, try Edinburgh bus station (0131 555 6363) or Glasgow (0141 333 3708) or for lost items on local buses, try Lothian buses' lost-property office in Annandale St.

Money

The basic unit of **currency** in the UK is the pound sterling (£), divided into 100 pence (p). Coins come in denominations of 1p, 2p, 5p, 10p, 20p, 50p, £1 and £2. Bank of England £5, £10, £20 and £50 banknotes are legal tender in Scotland; in addition the **Bank of Scotland (HBOS)**, the **Royal Bank of Scotland** (RBS) and the **Clydesdale Bank** issue their own banknotes in all the same denominations, plus a £100 note. At the time of going to press, £1 was worth around $1.26, €1.15, Can$1.67, Aus$1.91 and NZ$2.08. For the most up-to-date exchange rates, check the useful website www.xe.com.

Credit/debit cards are by far the most convenient way to carry your money, and most hotels, shops and restaurants in Edinburgh accept the major brand cards. There are ATMs all over the city and every area has a branch of at least one of the big Scottish high-street **banks** and/or UK banks, usually with an ATM attached. General **banking hours** are Monday to Friday from 9 or 9.30am to 4 or 5pm, though some branches are open until slightly later on Thursdays. Post offices charge **no commission**, have longer opening hours, and are therefore often a good place to change money and cheques.

Opening hours

Traditional **shop hours** are Monday to Saturday 9am to 5.30 or 6pm, with many closing later on Thursdays or Fridays (around 9pm). Large supermarkets typically stay open till 8pm or 10pm and a few manage 24hr opening.

Phones

Public **payphones** are a rarity in Edinburgh, and seldom used. If you're taking your **mobile phone/cell phone** with you to Scotland, check with your service provider whether your phone will work abroad and what the call charges will be. Since Brexit, the UK is no longer be covered for free roaming under EU legislation, so check your network provider's policy on data roaming to avoid being stung with sky-high charges for using your

Historic Environment Scotland and National Trust for Scotland

Many of Scotland's most treasured sights come under the control of the privately run National Trust for Scotland (www.nts.org.uk) or the state-run Historic Environment Scotland (www.historic environment.scot); we've quoted "NTS" or "HES", respectively, for each site reviewed in this Guide. Both organizations charge an admission fee for most places, and these can be quite high.

If you think you'll be visiting more than half a dozen NTS properties, or more than a dozen HES ones, it's worth taking annual membership, which costs around £59 (HES) or £63 (NTS) and allows free admission to their properties. In addition, HES offers short-term "Explorer" passes (HES £44/7 days; child £26/7 days).

Eating out price codes

Each **restaurant** and **café** reviewed in this Guide is accompanied by a price category, based on the cost of a **two-course meal** (or similar) for one, including a non-alcoholic drink.

£ = under £20
££ = £20–30
£££ = £30–40
££££ = over £40

phone. Calls to destinations further afield are still unregulated and can be prohibitively expensive. Unless you have a tri-band phone, it's unlikely that a mobile bought for use in the **US** will work outside the States and vice versa. Mobiles in **Australia** and **New Zealand** generally use the same system as the UK so should work fine. Beware of premium-rate numbers, which are common for pre-recorded information services – and usually have the prefix 09.

Post

Most **post offices** are open Monday to Friday 9am–5.30pm and Saturday 9am–12.30pm.

Price codes

Accommodation and restaurant listings throughout this Guide are accompanied by a corresponding price code; see boxes, above and page 138.

Smoking

Smoking is banned in all indoor public spaces, including all cafés, pubs, restaurants, clubs and public transport. These restrictions often cover e-cigarettes.

Time

Greenwich Mean Time (GMT) – equivalent to Co-ordinated Universal Time (UTC) – is used from the end of October to the end of March; for the rest of the year, the country switches to **British Summer Time** (BST), one hour ahead of GMT.

Tipping

There are no fixed rules for tipping. If you think you've received good service, particularly in restaurants or cafés, you may want to leave a tip of ten percent of the total bill (unless service has already been included). It's not normal, however, to leave tips in pubs, although bar staff are sometimes offered drinks, which they may accept in the form of money.

Toilets

There's a surprisingly small number of public toilets in Edinburgh, and the figure is ever decreasing as the council sells them off. Both Waverley and Haymarket train stations, and Edinburgh bus station, have toilets, as do most department stores, free museums and galleries.

Tourist information

The official tourist board in Scotland is known as **VisitScotland** (www.visit scotland.com) and its flagship iCentre is at 249 High Street (daily 9.30am–5pm; 0131 473 3820). As well as reserving accommodation, you can book tours, buy tickets for sights (including multi-passes) and transport (including ferries if you're planning on heading on to the Highlands and Islands). For listings, *The List* (www.list.co.uk) and *The Skinny* (www. theskinny.co.uk) are both excellent and invaluable sources of upcoming events in Edinburgh and in-depth cultural analysis, particularly during the Festival when they ramp up coverage.

Chronology

c.142AD Romans establish a fort at Cramond, in the domain of the Celtic Votadini tribe.

c.400–700 The Gododdin – descendants of the Votadini – establish hillfort of Din Eidyn on Castle Rock.

c.638 Din Eidyn falls to the Kingdom of Northumbria and assumes the Old English suffix, "-burh".

c.973 Lothian formally granted to Kenneth II by English king Edgar the Peaceful.

c.1130 King David 1 grants Edinburgh royal burgh status.

1291–1314 Edinburgh falls into English hands during the first of the Wars of Scottish Independence.

1320 The Declaration of Arbroath, asserting Scottish independence, is sent to the Pope.

1329 Robert The Bruce grants Edinburgh a new charter with jurisdiction over the port of Leith, allowing the city to prosper from foreign trade and establish itself as Scotland's permanent capital.

c.1365 Low Countries-born chronicler Froissart describes Edinburgh as "the Paris of Scotland".

c.1513 Work begins on Edinburgh's defensive Flodden Wall after the Scots are defeated by the English at the Battle of Flodden Field.

c.1544 Edinburgh is sacked and burned by the forces of Henry VIII after Scotland resists his attempt to marry off his son to Mary, Queen of Scots.

1560 Siege of Leith by English troops in alliance with Scottish Protestants ends in the Treaty of Edinburgh, the dissolution of Scotland's long-standing mutual defence pact with France (aka the Auld Alliance) and the establishment of Protestantism as Scotland's official religion.

1561 Mary, Queen of Scots lands in Leith after thirteen years in French exile, entering a cauldron of religious and political turmoil.

1567 Mary is forced to abdicate after a disastrous reign at Holyrood Palace, including the infamous murders of her secretary David Rizzio and consort Lord Darnley, with Reformation leader John Knox calling for her execution.

1603 Mary's son and heir James VI of Scotland becomes James I of England and Ireland with the Union of the Crowns.

1650 Edinburgh is occupied by English Puritan Oliver Cromwell after the Battle of Dunbar.

1651 English Parliament passes the Tender of Union, effectively annexing Scotland and dissolving the Scottish Parliament in Edinburgh.

1661 Re-institution of the Scottish Parliament following the restoration of Charles II.

1689 Scottish Parliament passes the Claim of Right act, asserting Charles' son, James VII's forfeiture of the Scottish throne and paving the way for a Presbyterian Church of Scotland.

1707 The Scottish Parliament is dissolved as Scotland signs the Act of Union with England, partly in response to the 1705 Alien Act, which had rendered Scots in England as foreign nationals, and placed an embargo on Scottish imports into English colonies; English spy Daniel Defoe reports on the violent and overwhelming opposition to the union.

1745 James VII's grandson Charles Edward Stuart aka Bonnie Prince Charlie, enters Edinburgh to cheering crowds and occupies Holyrood Palace for over a month, proclaiming "....the pretended Union of these Kingdoms being now at an end".

1746 Stuart dynasty meets final defeat at Battle of Culloden.

Late 1740s–c.1800 Edinburgh gains international renown as the centre of the Scottish Enlightenment, led by such revered thinkers as David Hume and Adam Smith.

1767 Work begins on the Georgian New Town as Edinburgh outgrows its medieval boundaries.

1867 Edinburgh City Improvement Act sees work commence on clearing Old Town slums.

1947 Edinburgh hosts its first International Festival.

1996 Danny Boyle's hugely acclaimed film adaptation of the Irvine Welsh novel, *Trainspotting*, accelerates the city's transformation into – and reclaiming its place as – one of the most dynamic, cosmopolitan and desirable cities in Europe.

1999 Scottish Devolution sees the reopening of the Scottish Parliament.

2008 The global financial crash and UK government bail-out of Royal Bank of Scotland dents Edinburgh's burgeoning financial sector and its rampant housing market.

2011 The Scottish National Party (SNP) win a majority at Holyrood and call a referendum on independence to be held in 2014.

2014 The No side wins 55 to 45 in the independence referendum.

2016 In the EU membership referendum, Scotland votes to remain 62 to 38, while the UK as a whole votes to leave.

2017 Scottish and Welsh governments excluded from Brexit negotiations; both reject the UK government's great repeal bill as a Westminster power grab.

2020 Britain leaves the EU just as the ruling SNP support surges.

2022 The SNP's push for a repeat of the 2014 independence referendum is rejected by Westminster. First Minister Nicola Sturgeon takes the issue to the UK Supreme Court, but judges rule she doesn't have the legal authority to hold a plebiscite without London's agreement. Sturgeon's "de facto" referendum strategy – where the SNP regard winning over 50 percent of Scottish votes in the next UK election as a mandate to negotiate separation with Westminster – meets opposition from her own party.

2023 Sturgeon resigns and is replaced by health secretary Humza Yousaf, who takes on the challenge of satisfying the Scottish National Party's hunger for independence as Westminster steadfastly opposes a second vote.

SMALL PRINT

Publishing Information

Third edition 2024

Distribution

UK, Ireland and Europe
Apa Publications (UK) Ltd; sales@roughguides.com
United States and Canada
Ingram Publisher Services; ips@ingramcontent.com
Australia and New Zealand
Booktopia; retailer@booktopia.com.au
Worldwide
Apa Publications (UK) Ltd; sales@roughguides.com

Special Sales, Content Licensing and CoPublishing

Rough Guides can be purchased in bulk quantities at discounted prices. We can create special editions, personalised jackets and corporate imprints tailored to your needs. sales@roughguides.com.
roughguides.com

Printed in China

This book was produced using **Typefi** automated publishing software.

Rough Guide Credits

Editor: Sarah Clark
Cartography: Katie Bennett
Picture editor: Tom Smyth
Layout: Pradeep Thapliyal

Original design: Richard Czapnik
Head of DTP and Pre-Press: Rebeka Davies
Head of Publishing: Sarah Clark

About the authors

Brendon Griffin has lived in Edinburgh for much of his adult life. When not wandering around Arthur's Seat, he writes for Rough Guides, tinkers with interior design, reviews Latin, African and Brazilian music and plays percussion (badly).

The 3rd edition of the *Pocket Rough Guide Edinburgh* was updated by Joanna Reeves, a Sussex-based travel writer for whom Scotland holds a special place in her heart – she even got engaged at a remote loch-side cabin in South Uist. She is the author of the 2nd edition of the *Pocket Rough Guide Isle of Skye and the Western Isles* and the editor of the *Rough Guide to the 100 Best Places in Scotland*.

Help us update

We've gone to a lot of effort to ensure that this edition of the **Pocket Rough Guide Edinburgh** is accurate and up-to-date. However, things change – places get "discovered", opening hours are notoriously fickle, restaurants and rooms raise prices or lower standards. If you feel we've got it wrong or left something out, we'd like to know, and if you can remember the address, the price, the hours, the phone number, so much the better.

Please send your comments with the subject line "**Pocket Rough Guide Edinburgh Update**" to mail@uk.roughguides.com. We'll acknowledge all contributions and send a copy of the next edition (or any other Rough Guide if you prefer) for the very best emails.

Photo Credits

(Key: T-top; C-centre; B-bottom; L-left; R-right)

Abi Radford/Timberyard 99
Alamy 106, 110, 111, 113, 119, 120, 122, 126
Courtesy of Jupiter Artland 129
Daniel Naczk 24C
David Bann 50
Douglas Macgilvray/Apa Publications 20B, 48, 54, 67, 96, 128, 132
Dr Neil's Garden Trust 14T
Edinburgh Festival Fringe 30
Edinburgh International Book Festival 29T
Edinburgh Jazz & Blues Festival 26
Edinburgh Printmakers 89
Edinburgh Science Festival 29B
Getty Images 44, 46, 52, 63, 64, 85, 105, 118, 136/137
iStock 15, 24T, 24B, 36, 43, 68, 71, 79, 80, 81, 95, 100, 117, 123, 124, 125, 131, 134, 135
Keith Inglis/Monteiths 51
Keth Valentine 32B

L'Escargot Bleu 92
Ludovic Farine 32T
Marc Millar/Kitchin 112
Mihaela Bodlovic 31
Mockford & Bonetti/Apa Publications 40
Picfair 102, 109, 127
Rhian McIntosh/The Caley Sample Room 121
Rocco Forte Hotels 83
Royal Edinburgh Military Tattoo 27T
Ruth Armstrong 27B
Scran & Scallie 104
Shutterstock 2TL, 2BL, 2C, 2BR, 4, 5, 6, 8, 12, 13T, 13B, 14B, 15, 16B, 16T, 18B, 18T, 19B, 19T, 20T, 20C, 21T, 21C, 21B, 22T, 22B, 23T, 23C, 23B, 25T, 25C, 25B, 35, 39, 41, 47, 49, 58, 61, 72, 73, 74, 75, 76, 78, 84, 90, 94, 103, 114, 115, 116, 133, 142/143
VisitScotland 1
VisitScotland/Kenny Lam 17B, 17T, 22C, 93

Cover Old Town shops **Jaroslav Moravcik/Shutterstock**

Index

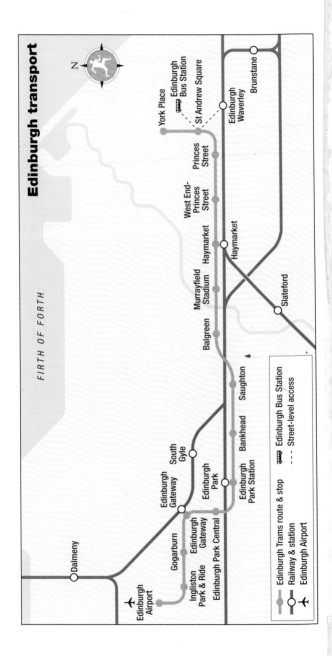

Edinburgh transport

FIRTH OF FORTH

N

- Edinburgh Airport
- Ingliston Park & Ride
- Gogarburn
- Edinburgh Gateway
- Edinburgh Park Central
- Edinburgh Park Station
- Bankhead
- Saughton
- Balgreen
- Murrayfield Stadium
- Haymarket
- West End–Princes Street
- Princes Street
- St Andrew Square
- York Place

South Gyle
Edinburgh Gateway
Edinburgh Park

Dalmeny
Haymarket
Slateford
Edinburgh Waverley
Brunstane
Edinburgh Bus Station

Edinburgh Trams route & stop
Railway & station
Edinburgh Airport
Edinburgh Bus Station
Street-level access